1-8

THE ATLANTIC MONTHLY
AND ITS MAKERS

JAMES RUSSELL LOWELL
First Editor of the *Atlantic Monthly*
1857–1861

THE
ATLANTIC MONTHLY
AND ITS MAKERS

BY

M. A. DeWOLFE HOWE

BOSTON

The ATLANTIC MONTHLY PRESS, Inc.

MDCCCCXIX

ACKNOWLEDGMENT

MANY of the following pages are derived freely from existing records of the *Atlantic Monthly* and the men who have made it. The files of the magazine itself have yielded much. Books of biography and reminiscence have also been drawn upon. For permission to do so acknowledgment is made to Messrs. Houghton Mifflin Co., by whom the following volumes have been published or acquired after publication: Edward Everett Hale's "James Russell Lowell and His Friends," Bliss Perry's "Park Street Papers," Thomas Wentworth Higginson's "Cheerful Yesterdays," Francis H. Underwood's biographies of Longfellow, Whittier, and Lowell; Horace E. Scudder's "James Russell Lowell," James T. Field's "Yesterdays with Authors," Ferris Greenslet's "Life of Thomas Bailey Aldrich," and Merwin's "Life of Bret Harte,"; and to Messrs. Harper and Brothers, publishers of Charles Eliot Norton's "Letters of James Russell Lowell," and William Dean Howells's "Literary Friends and Acquaintance" and "My Mark Twain." Messrs. Harper and Brothers have also kindly permitted the reproduction of contemporaneous wood cuts from *Harpers' Magazine*.

Boston, Massachusetts
November, Nineteen Eighteen

LIST OF ILLUSTRATIONS

EDITORS AND PUBLISHERS

Editors

I	James Russell Lowell	. . .	1857–1861
II	James Thomas Fields	. . .	1861–1871
III	William Dean Howells	. . .	1871–1881
IV	Thomas Bailey Aldrich	. . .	1881–1890
V	Horace Elisha Scudder	. . .	1890–1898
VI	Walter Hines Page	. . .	1898–1899
VII	Bliss Perry	. . .	1899–1909
VIII	Ellery Sedgwick	. . .	1909–

Publishers

I	Phillips, Sampson & Co.	. . .	1857–1859
II	Ticknor & Fields	. . .	1859–1867
III	Fields, Osgood & Co.	. . .	1868–1870
IV	James R. Osgood & Co.	. . .	1871–1873
V	H. O. Houghton & Co.	. . .	1874–1877
VI	Houghton, Osgood & Co.	. . .	1878–1879
VII	Houghton, Mifflin & Co.	. . .	1880–1908
VIII	Atlantic Monthly Co.	. . .	1908–

PREFATORY

WHEN THE ATLANTIC MONTHLY *reached its sixtieth birthday in its issue of November, 1917, it was older by six years than the oldest man concerned with the production of its first issue in November, 1857. This was Ralph Waldo Emerson, then fifty-four years old. Of the other eminent founders who accepted the invitation of the first publisher, Moses Dresser Phillips of the Boston firm of Phillips, Sampson & Co., to a dinner at the Parker House on May 5, 1857, to consider the establishment of a new literary and political magazine, Henry Wadsworth Longfellow, then fifty, stood next in point of age. Oliver Wendell Holmes was forty-eight; John Lothrop Motley, less identified with the magazine after its launching than any of the others, forty-three; James Russell Lowell, the first editor, thirty-eight; James Elliot Cabot, many years afterward the biographer of Emerson, thirty-six; and Francis H. Underwood, the "literary man" of Phillips, Sampson & Co., and the prime mover in the whole undertaking, but thirty-two.*

The ATLANTIC has long been a venerable institution. The writers who gave it first its high position stand in the public mind as the "venerable men" of American letters. Their ages in 1857 betoken the interesting fact that the ATLANTIC was never entirely a youthful experiment: it was planned and placed firmly on its feet by a remarkable group of men in or near the very prime of their great powers. The purpose of the following pages is to bring together from a variety of sources the chief facts regarding its beginnings and its growth to what it has become, illustrating these facts as freely as possible with passages of the personal record and remembrance which may impart to narrative something of the human quality which vitalizes the inner story of every institution.

THE ATLANTIC MONTHLY
AND ITS MAKERS

I

ON April 29, 1857, Longfellow wrote in his journal:
"Lowell was here last evening to interest me in a
new magazine, to be started in Boston by Phillips and Sampson. I told him I would write for it if I
wrote for any magazine." A week later the journal contained this entry: "Dined in town at Parker's, with
Emerson, Lowell, Motley, Holmes, Cabot, Underwood,
and the publisher, Phillips, to talk about the new magazine the last wishes to establish. It will no doubt be
done, though I am not so eager about it as the rest."
A more detailed account of this dinner is found in a
letter from Phillips himself, given in Edward Everett
Hale's " James Russell Lowell and His Friends ":—

I must tell you about a little dinner-party I gave about
two weeks ago. It would be proper, perhaps, to state that
the object, first, was to confer with my literary friends on
a somewhat extensive literary project, the particulars of
which I shall reserve till you come. But to the party: my
invitations included only R. W. Emerson, H. W. Longfellow, J. R. Lowell, Mr. Motley (the " Dutch Republic " man),
O. W. Holmes, Mr. Cabot, and Mr. Underwood, our literary
man. Imagine your uncle at the head of such a table, with
such guests. The above-named were the only ones invited,
and they were all present. We sat down at three P.M., and
arose at eight. The time occupied was longer by about
four hours and thirty minutes than I am in the habit of
consuming in that kind of occupation, but it was the rich-
est time intellectually by all odds that I have ever had.

RALPH WALDO EMERSON
From a crayon by Rowse in 1857, the year
of the founding.

Leaving myself and "literary man" out of the group, I think you will agree with me that it would be difficult to duplicate that number of such conceded scholarship in the whole country besides. Mr. Emerson took the first post of honor at my right, and Mr. Longfellow the second at my left. The exact arrangement of the table was as follows:—

Mr. UNDERWOOD

CABOT	LOWELL
MOTLEY	HOLMES
LONGFELLOW	EMERSON

PHILLIPS

They seemed so well pleased that they adjourned, and invited me *to meet them* again to-morrow, when I shall again meet the same persons, with one other (Whipple, the essayist) added to that brilliant constellation of the philosophical, poetical, and historical talent. Each one is known alike on both sides of the Atlantic, and is read beyond the limits of the English language. Though all this is known to you, you will pardon me for intruding it upon you. But still I have the vanity to believe that you will think them the most natural thoughts in the world to me. Though I say it that should not, it was the proudest moment of my life.

Dr. Hale added to this letter his own report of the words with which Phillips announced the plan of the magazine — a little speech which was apparently a matter of common knowledge at the time: "Mr. Cabot is much wiser than I am, Dr. Holmes can write funnier verses than I can, Mr. Motley can write history better than I, Mr. Emerson is a philosopher and I am not, Mr. Lowell knows more of the old poets than I, but none of you knows the American people as well as I do."

This may have been the truth. Whether it was or not, one cannot help wishing that in all the acknowledgments of superiority made by Phillips, either in his spoken words or in the letter so frankly revealing his satisfaction in the unwonted company in which he found himself, he had given Underwood credit for being something more than "our literary man." Professor Bliss Perry, in an article in the Fiftieth Anniversary number of the *Atlantic*, now included in his volume of "Park Street Papers," defined Underwood far more accurately as "The Editor who was never the Editor." He was indeed something more than that — he was the *fons et origo* of the entire enterprise. Of Massachusetts birth (in 1825), Underwood, after a period of study in Amherst College, had lived in Kentucky, where a native repugnance to slavery had become a militant antipathy to it. Returning to Massachusetts in 1850, he interested himself in the Free Soil movement, was appointed in 1852 Clerk of the State Senate, and by 1853 had persuaded the publishing firm of J. P. Jewett & Co. to stand behind him in the establishing of a new magazine.

These publishers had issued "Uncle Tom's Cabin," which Phillips, Sampson & Co. had refused for fear of alienating their Southern customers; and it was only natural that J. P. Jewett, the head of the house, should see eye to eye with Underwood in his vision of a periodical which should unite the strongest forces of expression in the joined cause of letters and reform. As early, therefore, as 1853 — four years before the first issue of the *Atlantic* — Underwood is found in active correspondence with the chief writers of the country, especially the outstanding New England group, in the interest of a magazine to make its initial appearance at the beginning of 1854. There was a cordial response, not only in promises but in manuscripts, and there was every expectation that the dream would become a reality, with Underwood at the helm of the new venture, when, near the end of 1853, the Jewett firm met with no less a misfortune than failure.

It was a sad business for Underwood, to whom Lowell wrote, December 5, 1853 : "The explosion of one of these castles in Spain sometimes sprinkles dust on all the rest of our lives ; but I hope you are of better heart, and will rather look upon the affair as a burning of your ships which only makes victory the more imperative." So it seems indeed to have been with him. From his association with the Jewett project, Underwood passed to the publishing office of Phillips, Sampson & Co. It was, however, not until 1857 that he could persuade the cautious Phillips to take up the project which Jewett had been obliged to drop. He might not have succeeded then, but that Mrs. Stowe, whose "Dred" Phillips had been bold enough to publish in 1856, added her persuasions to Underwood's. Her influence was potent. Its exercise was followed by the dinner already chronicled. Though Underwood, in his employer's eyes, cut but an obscure figure at it, the gathering would hardly have taken place but for his imagination and enthusiasm, to say nothing of his personal relations of friendship with Lowell and others hitherto outside the immediate circle of Phillips himself. "The Editor who was never the Editor" has received his full recognition only in later years. At the beginning he was content, after doing all the work preliminary to the establishment of the *Atlantic,* to nominate its first editor, and to serve as his office assistant.

This editor was James Russell Lowell. His previous slight editorial experience, with the short-lived *Pioneer* and the *Anti-Slavery Standard,* of which he had been a corresponding editor, was a smaller qualification for the post than his acknowledged position as poet, scholar, and man of letters. He never showed the instincts of a good editor more truly than by insisting as "a condition precedent" to accepting the editorship that Oliver Wendell Holmes should be engaged as the first contributor. Holmes at that time had written but little that gave definite promise of the place his "Autocrat" and the succeeding "Breakfast-Table" papers were to give him. Many years later he wrote: "I think therefore that the *Atlantic* came for my fruit just as it was ripe to gathering, but I never knew it was so until afterwards." Lowell appears to have known it in advance.

Besides standing as the one indispensable contributor, Dr. Holmes had the important function of naming the magazine. Many titles were in the air. J. T. Trowbridge wrote to Underwood: "If the 'American Monthly' will not do, what do you say to the 'Anglo-American'?" Emerson suggested "Town and Country," presumably in relation to a "Town and Country Club" to which he and many of his circle had belonged.

Other titles [wrote Arthur Gilman in the *Atlantic* of November, 1907] had been suggested, but none proved at once satisfactory. Dr. Holmes told me that one day after he had retired to "his virtuous couch," he suddenly roused himself and exclaimed to his wife: "I have it! It shall be called *The Atlantic Monthly Magazine!* Soon you'll hear the boys crying through the streets, ' Here's your *Atlantic, 'tlantic, 'tlantic, 'tlantic!* '" *Atlantic* it became, but the publishers dropped the word "magazine," and were sufficiently upbraided by the word-mongers for their stupidity in making a noun of an adjective, although " Monthly " had been used in England, perhaps for a hundred years, in the same way.

It is a genial circumstance that most of the decisions regarding the early courses of the *Atlantic* were taken at dinner-tables. Longfellow's journal records a second dinner for the discussion of the magazine project before it was definitely adopted; and in Pickard's "Life of Whittier" the following passage is found:—

At a dinner given by Mr. Phillips, the publisher, in the summer of 1857, there were present Longfellow, Emerson, Whittier, Lowell, Holmes, Motley, Edmund Quincy, and other critics of high reputation. The plans for the new magazine were discussed and arranged at this dinner. Mr. Underwood nominated Lowell as Editor-in-chief, and his name was received with enthusiasm. Holmes suggested the name *The Atlantic Monthly.* The success of the enterprise was assured from the start, and a new era in American literature was established.

Many other dinners marked these early days — generally at the Parker House, once at Fontarive's restaurant in Winter Place, where the host, " a quaint and delightful artist in his way," according to Underwood, "produced a menu worthy of Lucullus." Still another dinner took place at the famous North Cambridge tavern kept by one Porter, whose name long survived in " Porter's Station," and is even associated in local etymology with the Porterhouse steak of national fame. On this occasion the host made the answer, embalmed in Dr. Holmes's verse, to the query what is left of a goose when the breast and legs are taken:—

And Landlord Porter, with uplifted eyes,
Smiles on the simple querist and replies,
" When from a goose you've taken legs and breast,
Wipe lips, thank God, and leave the poor the rest."

At Porter's the ancient secret of making flip survived, and there is an envious legend that the poets and sages who attended this dinner made zig-zag homeward tracks in the snow that had fallen while they sat at the board. This legend is refuted, but not the other that, as they walked to Cambridge, the younger members of the party chanted the East Indian ballad:—

> "This is a Rajah!
> Putterum!"

And there is no occasion to challenge Underwood's excellent bit of reminiscence: "Every one was in supreme good humor. The Medical Professor shone with an easy superiority, and tossed about his compliments like juggler's balls. Being particularly gracious towards Longfellow, and having just written that authors were like cats, sure to purr when stroked the right way of the fur, Longfellow, with a merry twinkle in his eyes, interrupted him with 'I purr, I purr!'"

There were so many other meetings of the publishers, editors, and contributors, in celebration of the monthly appearance of the magazine, that a loosely organized "Atlantic Club" came into a brief being. This has been confused with the vigorously surviving Saturday Club, which had its origin at about the same time and contained many of the same members; but they were in reality distinct. In T. W. Higginson's "Cheerful Yesterdays" there is a description of one of the most memorable meetings of the Atlantic Club, so pleasantly charged with the spirit of the time that it must be quoted entire:—

During the first year of the magazine under Phillips & Sampson's management, these were monthly dinners, in or near Boston, under the generalship of Francis H. Underwood, the office editor, and John C. Wyman, then his assistant. The most notable of these gatherings was undoubtedly that held at the Revere House, on the occasion of Mrs. Stowe's projected departure for Europe. It was the only one to which ladies were invited, and the invitation was accepted with a good deal of hesitation by Mrs. Stowe, and with a distinct guarantee that no wine should be furnished for the guests. Other feminine contributors were invited, but for various reasons no ladies appeared except Mrs. Stowe and Miss Harriet Prescott (now Mrs. Spofford), who had already won fame by a story called "In a Cellar," the scene of which was laid in Paris, and which was so thoroughly French in all its appointments that it was suspected of being a translation from that language, although much inquiry failed to reveal the supposed original. It may be well to add that the honest young author had so little appreciation of the high compliment thus paid her that she indignantly proposed to withdraw her manuscript in consequence. These two ladies arrived promptly, and the gentlemen were kept waiting, not greatly to their minds, in the hope that other fair contributors would appear. When at last it was decided to proceed without further delay, Dr. Holmes and I were detailed to escort the ladies to the dining-room: he as head of the party, and I as the only one that knew the younger lady. As we went upstairs the vivacious Autocrat said to me, "Can I venture it? Do you suppose that Mrs. Stowe disapproves of me very much?" he being then subject to severe criticism from the more conservative theologians. The lady was gracious, however, and seemed glad to be rescued at last from her wearisome waiting. She came downstairs wearing a green wreath, of which Longfellow says in his diary (July 9, 1859) that he "thought it very becoming."

We seated ourselves at table, Mrs. Stowe at Lowell's right, and Miss Prescott at Holmes's, I next to her, Ed-

W. PHILLIPS SARGENT BARTOL   CRANCH WEISS H. JAMES, SR.
                                              HOLMES WHITTIER
                                                      T. W. HIGGINSON

A Radical Club meeting at the house of the Rev. John T. Sargent,
13 Chestnut Street, attended by *Atlantic* contributors.

mund Quincy next to me. Dr. Stowe was at Holmes's left,
Whittier at his; and Longfellow, Underwood, John Wyman, and others were present. I said at once to Miss Prescott, "This is a new edition of "Evelina, or a Young Lady's
Entrance into the World.' Begin at the beginning: what
did you and Mrs. Stowe talk about for three quarters of
an hour?" She answered demurely, "Nothing, except that
she once asked me what o'clock it was, and I told her I
didn't know." There could hardly be a better illustration
of the curious mixture of *mauvaise honte* and indifference
which often marred the outward manners of this remarkable woman. It is very likely that she had not been introduced to her companion, and perhaps had never heard her
name; but imagine any kindly or gracious person of middle age making no effort to relieve the shyness of a young
girl stranded with herself during three quarters of an
hour of enforced seclusion!

The modest entertainment proceeded; conversation set
in, but there was a visible awkwardness, partly from the
presence of two ladies, one of whom was rather silent by
reason of youth, and the other by temperament; and moreover, the thawing influence of wine was wanting. There
were probably no men of the party, except Whittier and
myself, who did not habitually drink it, and various little
jokes began to circle *sotto voce* at the table; a suggestion
for instance, from Longfellow, that Miss Prescott might
be asked to send down into her Cellar for the wine she had
described so well, since Mrs. Stowe would allow none
above stairs. Soon, however, a change came over the aspect of affairs. My neighbor on the right, Edmund Quincy,
called a waiter mysteriously, and giving him his glass of
water remained tranquilly while it was being replenished.
It came back suffused with a rosy hue. Some one else followed his example, and presently the "conscious water"
was blushing at various points around the board, although
I doubt whether Holmes, with water-drinkers two deep
on each side of him, got half his share of the coveted bev-

erage. If he had, it might have modified the course of his talk, for I remember that he devoted himself largely to demonstrating to Dr. Stowe that all swearing doubtless originated in the free use made by the pulpit of sacred words and phrases; while Lowell, at the other end of the table, was maintaining for Mrs. Stowe's benefit that "Tom Jones" was the best novel ever written. This line of discussion may have been lively, but was not marked by eminent tact; and Whittier, indeed, told me afterwards that Dr. and Mrs. Stowe agreed in saying to him that, while the company at the club was no doubt distinguished, the conversation was not quite what they had been led to expect. Yet Dr. Stowe was of a kindly nature and perhaps was not seriously disturbed even when Holmes assured him that there were in Boston whole families not perceptibly affected by Adam's fall; as, for instance, the family of Ware.

From this long and slightly premature digression it is time to turn back and look with some care at the first issue of the magazine, dated November, 1857, and appearing late in October. Ten of the fourteen authors who made the principal contributions to it were Motley, Longfellow, Emerson, Charles Eliot Norton, Holmes, Whittier, Mrs. Stowe, J. T. Trowbridge, Lowell, and Parke Godwin. Whittier's contribution was his poem, "Tritemius," Longfellow's his "Santa Filomena," in praise of Florence Nightingale, who had recently shown in the Crimea, for the first time, what nursing might contribute to war. Lowell contributed his sonnet, "The Maple," his characteristic rhymes on "The Origin of Didactic Poetry," and, in an editorial "Round Table," the graceful prose setting for some verses of Holmes to Motley on his departure for Europe. Emerson gave, besides the essay "Illusions," four poems, "The Rommany Girl," "The Chartist's Complaint,"

" Days," and " Brahma." The supremely felicitous word " hyprocritic," in the first line of " Days," — the little poem which alone would have secured a permanent place for Emerson in American literature, — resulted from a suggestion of Lowell's that the poet's original word " hypercritical " did not say precisely what he meant. (It should be said in passing that, in the second issue, Whittier's " Skipper Ireson's Ride " owed the Marblehead flavor of its

> "Here's Flud Oirson, fur his horrd horrt,
> Torr'd an' futherr'd an' corr'd in a corrt,"

to Lowell's keen ear for New England dialect and a corresponding suggestion accepted by Whittier.) Mrs. Stowe and Trowbridge were represented in the first issue by short stories; and there was the first installment of " The Autocrat of the Breakfast-Table." All the articles were unsigned, and it is no wonder that every one asked himself and his neighbor who this Autocrat might be with his offhand introduction, " I was just going to say when I was interrupted "; for there could not have been one reader in a thousand who recalled that in the old *New England Magazine* for 1831 and 1832 there were two papers of an " Autocrat of the Breakfast-Table " by a young student of medicine; and the whimsicality of going on after an interruption of twenty-five years would have puzzled even the knowing ones of a generation that had not yet learned the Breakfast-Table habit of thought.

Emerson's characteristic justification of the practice of anonymity was that " the names of contributors will be given out when the names are worth more than the articles." Motley wrote to Holmes, apropos of the contributors to an early issue: " Doubtless I shall know them all by the ' twinkling of their eyes.' " Indeed, the authorship was evidently an open secret in many quarters. Norton made no scruple of telling Clough in a letter of 25 October, 1857, who were the chief contributors to the first number. Even the Boston correspondent of the Springfield *Republican* was able to send his paper immediately an ascription of all the articles in this issue to their several writers. Through the first eight volumes — four years — the authors' names were not printed, even in the semi-annual index. The practice of printing them there began in the ninth volume; not until the twenty-sixth (1870) was the present usage of attaching the authors' names to all but editorial contributions begun.

The magazine inevitably scored an immediate success. There were of course other periodicals at the time, in New York and Philadelphia, but no one of them, either in personnel of contributors, amounting virtually to a " staff," or in controlling purposes, could engage in a serious rivalry with the *Atlantic*. *The Knickerbocker, Putnam's,* and the Philadelphia magazines of the period are now long vanished. Writing retrospectively in 1882, Underwood said:—

Of the purely literary magazines still existing, we can remember only *Harper's* that was successful then. But in 1857, and before that time, *Harper's* was largely filled with copied articles, and neither that nor any other literary periodical was an outspoken organ of opinion. It was then supposed necessary to avoid controverted topics, and epicene literature was mostly in vogue. Writers and thinkers might deplore this, but publishers were timid, and kept a weather eye open to watch the vanes of public opinion. The *Atlantic Monthly* was started with the definite purpose of concentrating the efforts of the best writers upon literature and politics, under the light of the highest morals.

Two years later Underwood wrote in his biography of Whittier: "The *Atlantic* was intended, first of all, to be entertaining; but every number contained a political article by Parke Godwin or by Lowell, and the public understood and felt that this was the point of the ploughshare that was to break up the old fields." The magazine's own definition of its political aim, on the back cover of its first issue, read as follows:—

In politics, the *Atlantic* will be the organ of no party or clique, but will honestly endeavor to be the exponent of what its conductors believe to be the American idea. It will deal frankly with persons and with parties, endeavoring always to keep in view that moral element which transcends all persons and parties, and which alone makes the basis of a true and lasting national prosperity. It will not rank itself with any sect of anties: but with that body of men which is in favor of Freedom, National Progress, and Honor, whether public or private.

In the same pronouncement of aims the publishers declared, with special reference to Literature, that "while native writers will receive the most solid encouragement, and will be mainly relied upon to fill the pages of the *Atlantic,* they will not hesitate to draw from the foreign forces at their command, as occasion may require, relying rather on the competency of an author to treat a particular subject, than on any other claim whatever." The "native writers" were at first chiefly natives of New England; and, though not to be ranked "with any sect of anties," were of that body of men whose belief in freedom implied a strong corresponding disbelief in slavery. "This group of writers," wrote T. W. Higginson in his "Cheerful Yesterdays," "was doubtless a local product; but so is every new variety of plum or pear which the gardener finds in his garden. He does not quarrel with it for having made its appearance in some inconvenient corner instead of in the centre, nor does he think it unpardonable that it did not show itself everywhere at once; the thing of importance is that it has arrived."

The *Atlantic* had no greater good fortune in its beginnings than that Lowell was its editorial chief gardener. The public knew him for what verily he was — so true and spirited a patriot that no fear of consequences withheld him from open identification with the heterodox cause of anti-slavery; so genuine a poet, so penetrating a critic, so sound a scholar, that in all the portions of his editorial field his word was the word of authority. One likes perhaps best of all the fun he found in his labors, at least until they became too onerous for him. His pet name "Maga" for the magazine implied in itself even a sort of tolerance for the "pen-and-inkubus" which an irksome contributor might become, or for the critic to whom he felt "inclined to apply the quadrisyllabic name of the brother of Agis, King of Sparta" — a Grecian character whom Felton was learned enough to identify as Eudamidas. It is pleasant to find him writing, in the earliest days of his editorship, about the compensations of the magazine: —

First, it has almost got me out of debt, and next, it compels me into morning walks to the printing office. There is a little foot-path which leads along the river bank, and it is lovely; whether in clear, cold mornings, when the fine filaments of the bare trees on the horizon seem floating up like sea-masses in the ether sea, or when (as yesterday) a gray mist fills our Cambridge cup and gives a doubtful loom to its snowy brim of hills, while the silent gulls wheel over the rustling cakes of ice which the Charles is whirling seaward.

Of one of his morning walks to his editorial work Trowbridge has told the following story, bearing upon Lowell's dealings with rejected manuscripts: —

He was walking one windy morning over Cambridge bridge, when his hat blew off, and fell into the Charles, with half a dozen or more manuscripts with which it was freighted, and which he was returning to the Boston office. A boatman recovered the hat, but the scattered manuscripts perished in those waves of oblivion. "If they had been accepted articles," Lowell remarked, "it wouldn't have been quite so bad; for we might with some grace ask the writers for fresh copies. But how can you tell a self-respecting contributor that his manuscript has been not only rejected, but sent to a watery grave!"

There are many evidences, besides such words as these and the fortunate editing of Emerson's and Whittier's lines to which allusion has already been made, that Lowell dealt helpfully with his contributors. That he also dealt loyally with them appears in his backing up of Dr. Holmes under the attacks of the evangelical press. The " Autocrat " papers had rendered him clearly suspect on questions of orthodoxy in religion. The " Professor " called forth violent condemnation. " If you could believe many of the newspapers," wrote Horace E. Scudder in his biography of Lowell, " Dr. Holmes was a sort of reincarnation of Voltaire, who stood for the most audacious enemy of Christianity in modern times." It was thus that Lowell wrote to him on the

appearance of the first installment of "The Professor": "The religious press (a true sour-cider press
with belly-ache privileges attached) will be at you, but
after smashing one of them you will be able to furnish
yourself with a Sampson's weapon for the rest of the
Philisterei."

Many such weapons would have been needed to safe-
guard the *Atlantic* as a whole at this time. Of the very
first number one of the sectarian papers, published in
Boston, said, "We shall observe the progress of the
work not without solicitude." Their watchfulness was
soon rewarded in a measure, for of the third number
they declared, "The only objectionable article is one
by Emerson on 'Books,' in which the sage of Concord
shows his customary disregard of the religious opinions
of others and of the fundamental laws of social moral-
ity." The next month it was a little better: "With the
exception of a slur at the doctrine of eternal retribu-
tion, in the Literary Notices, we do not recall anything
really exceptionable in its pages." The curious reader
may find the slur in a single sentence of Dr. Holmes's
review of Mrs. Lee's "Parthenia" — a sentence which,
aside from its great length, has nothing astonishing
about it except the fact that sixty years ago its senti-
ments could not pass unchallenged.

But of course it was the writings of Dr. Holmes
which gave the vigilant defenders of orthodoxy the
greatest concern. In a letter written to Motley in 1861
Holmes exclaimed: "But oh! such a belaboring as I
have had from the so-called 'Evangelical' press for the
last two or three years, almost without intermission!
There must be a great deal of weakness and rottenness
when such extreme bitterness is called out by such a
good-natured person as I can claim to be in print."

Even the New York *Independent,* which was printing every week the sermons of Henry Ward Beecher, said of " The Professor at the Breakfast-Table " when it appeared as a book:—

We presume that we do but speak the general conviction, as it certainly is our own, when we say that that which was to have been apprehended has not been avoided by the "Professor," but has been painfully realized in his new series of utterances. He has dashed at many things which he does not understand, has succeeded in irritating and repelling from the magazine many who had formerly read it with pleasure, and has neither equaled the spirit and vigorous vivacity, nor maintained the reputation, shown and acquired by the preceding papers. It would have been better for all concerned if the pen of the "Autocrat" had never been resumed by a hand wearied with its previous work, and a mind made almost comically self-sufficient and dogmatical by an unexpected measure of literary success.

Writing of these papers nearly twenty-five years after their first publication, Dr. Holmes himself said: " It amuses me to look back on some of the attacks they called forth. Opinions which do not excite the faintest show of temper in this time from those who do not accept them were treated as if they were the utterances of a Nihilist incendiary. It required the exercise of some forbearance not to recriminate."

Lowell's editorship of the *Atlantic* was next to the shortest of all the eight which have spanned its history of more than sixty years. It lasted but four years, ending in 1861. By that time he had become somewhat weary of its necessarily exacting routine, but he had laid the enduring foundations which owed much of their

CHARLES ELIOT NORTON

Contributor to the first issue of the *Atlantic* and
to its Fiftieth Anniversary Number.

permanence to the spirit behind his words: " A part of
the magazine as long as I have anything to do with it,
shall be expressly *not* for the mob (of well-dressed gentlemen who read with ease)." How permanent the
structure was to be, he could not have imagined, any
more than his friend Norton, writing from Paris on
June 8, 1857, when he first heard of the plans for the
new periodical, and characteristically went to work at
once to help the editor, as he did with great success, in
securing valuable contributions from English writers.

Of course [said Norton] it will succeed with you as its
Editor, and with such liberal arrangements for its beginning. But such things are never permanent in our country. They burn brightly for a little while, and then burn
out, — and some other light takes their place. It would be
a great thing for us if any undertaking of this kind could
live long enough to get affections and associations connected with it, whose steady glow should take the place of,
and more than supply, the shine of novelty, and the dazzle
of a first go-off. I wish we had a Sylvanus Urban a hundred and fifty years old. I wish, indeed, we had anything
so old in America; I would give a thousand of our new
lamps for the one old, battered, but true magical light.

Both Lowell and Norton lived to see a long step in the
direction of this faithful friend's desire.

How many years Lowell might have retained the
editorship of the magazine if its publication had not
changed hands, it is impossible to say. But in 1859
both Phillips and Sampson died, and their firm was
dissolved. The *Atlantic* was then purchased by the
firm of Ticknor & Fields, and Underwood's editorial
connection with it ceased. Lowell held his post for two
years longer under the new employers, when considera-

tions of office economy played their part in the transfer of the editorship to the well-qualified hands of James T. Fields, the "literary" member of the firm. When these publishers acquired the magazine, Fields himself was in Europe, and the circumstances of the purchase, related in a "Contributors' Club" paper in the *Atlantic* of November, 1907, were curiously haphazard in character. This is the story there given: —

You remember that in its extreme youth the magazine was transferred from the publishing house of Phillips and Sampson, to whose enterprise it owed its existence, to that of Ticknor and Fields, then occupying the "Old Corner Bookstore," on School Street, just a little farther down than the Old South Church. The late Governor Alexander H. Rice told me on that November evening [of a meeting described by the writer] how the transfer was made. The original publishers had failed, and Mr. Rice was their assignee, upon whom rested the responsibility of settling the business. The *Atlantic* was a valuable part of the assets, of course, and Mr. Rice said that he sent letters to a dozen different publishers telling them that he would sell it to the highest bidder whose offer should be received by noon on a certain day. The day arrived, and not one bid had come. Mr. Rice walked out to the office of Ticknor and Fields, and said to Mr. Ticknor, "I have not yet received your bid for the *Atlantic*." "No," replied the publishers, "and you will not, for we don't care to undertake the responsibility of the venture." In point of fact, Mr. Rice told me, the risk was not great, for the circulation at the time stood at thirty thousand copies.

Mr. Rice was not to be put off in this cavalier fashion. He pointed to the clock on the Old South, and it was after half-past eleven. "I am about to go to my office to open the bids," said he, "and I am sure that Ticknor and Fields will be sorry if I find none there from them." Mr. Ticknor

was apparently immovable. Mr. Fields was in Europe.
Mr. Rice continued his appeals. The hands of the old
clock kept on their way, and soon they indicated five minutes of twelve. Then Mr. Rice made his last effort, and
Mr. Ticknor turned to his desk and wrote a line on a piece
of paper, handing it to the governor, sealed. Mr. Rice
carried it to his office, and solemnly proceeded to open it.
It was the only bid, and the sum mentioned was ten thousand dollars. Mr. Rice went at once to Mr. Ticknor again,
and said, " The *Atlantic* is yours! " Mr. Ticknor was
startled, and replied, " Pray let no one know what I bid,
for all my friends would think me crazy! " The brilliant
history of the magazine, during this period of the ownership by the honored house of Ticknor and Fields shows at
once how little publishers are able to forecast the future
and how difficult it is to estimate the value of literary
assets. Doubtless Mr. Ticknor thought, when he handed
his little slip of paper to Governor Rice, that he had made
a bid so modest that he was in no danger of having it accepted; and it seems equally sure that, when he found no
other publisher had bid so high as he, he was alarmed
lest he had made a deplorable exhibition of a lack of
business acumen.

Another rendering of the transfer of the magazine
appears in Scudder's biography of Lowell. " There was
a lively competition," he says, " among publishers to
secure the magazine. The Harpers purposed to buy it,
to suppress their rival, it was said; there were offers
from Philadelphia, and some of the younger men connected with the firm of Phillips and Sampson made an
effort to establish a new firm which should buy the
whole business of Phillips and Sampson, including the
magazine."

In any event Lowell's editorship would have come
to an end about when it did. His cheerful acceptance

Messrs W. D. Ticknor & Co.

in a/c with the Assignees of

Phillips Sampson & Co.

1859 Octr 17	For	Stereotyp'd Plates back Nos Good will &c &c of the Atlantic Monthly	10,000.00
20	"	paid J. R. Lowell	205.00
"	"	" Mrs Stowe for Novr & Decr Nos	400.00
Novr 30	"	" George Nichols	51.67
	"	" Sundry Contributors	494.67
Octr 17	"	Rice Kendall & Co. bill for Paper	2002.00
"	"	M. M. Chick " Binding	311.50
"	"	H. O. Houghton & Co. " Stereotyping Comp.	293.88
	"	Saml Chism " Printing	301.55
	"	Bill of Paper Machine &c	40.66
	"	14 8/20 Rms Cover Paper @ 6.7	92.40
			14,193.33

Cr

1859 Novr 30	By	Amt paid Contributors 494.67			
	"	Their Note Octr 17/59	3 ms	833.33	
	"	" " " " d/o	4 "	833.33	
	"	" " " " d/o	5 "	833.34	
	"	" " " " d/o	6 "	833.33	
	"	" " " " d/o	7 "	833.33	
	"	" " " " d/o	8 "	833.34	
	"	" " " " d/o	9 "	833.33	
	"	" " " " d/o	10 "	833.33	
	"	" " " " d/o	11 "	833.33	
	"	" " " " d/o	12 "	833.34	
	"	" " " " d/o	13 "	833.33	
	"	" " " " d/o	14 "	833.34	
	"	" " " " 24/o	3 "	456.67	
	"	" " " " d/o	6 "	2002.00	
	"	" " " Novr 17/o	6 "	1039.99	14,193.33

E. & O. E.

Recd Payment as above

A. H. Rice } Assignees

H. Sewell

of the situation was made clear in a letter of May 23, 1861, to his successor in the editorial chair :—

My dear Fields,—I wish you all joy of your work. You will find it no bad apprenticeship or prelude for that warmer and more congenial world to which all successful booksellers are believed by devout authors to go. I was going to say I was glad to be rid of my old man of the sea. But I don't believe I am. I doubt if we see the finger of Providence so readily in the stoppage of a salary as in its beginning or increment. A bore, moreover, that is periodical gets a friendly face at last and we miss it on the whole. Even the gout men don't like to have stop too suddenly, lest it may have struck to the stomach.

Well, good-by, delusive royalty! I abdicate with what grace I may. I lay aside my paper crown and feather sceptre. I have been at least no Bourbon — if I have not learned much, I have forgotten a great deal. . . .

You will be surprised before long to find how easily you get on without me, and wonder that you ever thought me a necessity. It is amazing how quickly the waters close over one. He carries down with him the memory of his splash and struggle, and fancies it is still going on when the last bubble even has burst long ago. Good-by. Nature is equable. I have lost the *Atlantic,* but my cow has calved as if nothing had happened.

JAMES T. FIELDS
Second Editor of the *Atlantic Monthly*
1861–1871

II

The second editor of the *Atlantic,* James Thomas Fields, held in the world of letters no such commanding place as Lowell's. Yet he held a distinctive and important place, and contributed through the ten years of his editorship — 1861 to 1871 — the special element of variety and strength which a publisher of the widest possible acquaintance and sympathies could bring to the pages of his periodical; for it should be said that, excepting the present editor, Fields has been the only one who was also a publisher of the magazine, and thus responsible for both its literary and its business success.

Among publishers Fields stood quite alone. In all the annals of American commerce in books there is no other such instance of a man who combined in his own person the offices of friendship and of business. His warm personal friends, who valued him equally for what he was and for what he did in their interest, were the remarkable company of writers in England as in America, who gave especially to the third quarter of the nineteenth century its "Augustan" quality in letters. Born in Portsmouth, New Hampshire, Fields came to Boston in 1831, as a fourteen-year-old boy-of-all-work in a bookstore. He seized every opportunity of improving his mind, and even by the time he was twenty-one received recognition as a local poet. As a bookseller, John Fiske related of him that "in his youth he used to surprise his fellow clerks by divining beforehand what kind of a book was likely to be wanted by any chance customer that entered the store." As time went on, the Old Corner Bookstore, with which he was identified, became a notable Boston

institution. The place and the man who made it what
it was were thus described by George William Curtis,
in *Harper's Monthly*, soon after Fields's death in 1881:

THE " OLD CORNER BOOKSTORE "
Corner of Washington and School Streets, 1880.

The annals of publishing and the traditions of publishers in this country will always mention the little Corner
Book-Store in Boston as you turn out of Washington
Street into School Street, and those who recall it in other
days will always remember the curtained desk at which
poet and philosopher and historian and divine, and the
doubting, timid, young author, were sure to see the bright
face and to hear the hearty welcome of James T. Fields.
What a crowded, busy shop it was, with the shelves full of
books, and piles of books upon the counters and tables,
and loiterers tasting them with their eyes, and turning
the glossy new pages — loiterers at whom you looked curiously, suspecting them to be makers of books as well as

readers. You knew that you might be seeing there in the
flesh and in common clothes the famous men and women
whose genius and skill made the old world a new world
for every one upon whom their spell lay. Suddenly, from
behind the green curtain, came a ripple of laughter, then
a burst, a chorus; gay voices of two or three or more, but
always of one — the one who sat at the desk and whose
place was behind the curtain, the literary partner of the
house, the friend of the celebrated circle which has made
the Boston of the middle of this century as justly re-
nowned as the Edinburgh of the close of the last century,
the Edinburgh that saw Burns, but did not know him.
That curtained corner in the Corner Book-Store is remembered by those who knew it in its great days, as Beau-
mont recalled the revels at the immortal tavern: —

> What things have we seen
> Done at the Mermaid! heard words that have been
> So nimble and so full of subtle flame,
> As if that every one from whence they came
> Had meant to put his whole wit in a jest!

What merry peals! What fun and chaff and story! Not
only the poet brought his poem there still glowing from
his heart, but the lecturer came from the train with his
freshest touches of local humor. It was the exchange of
wit, the Rialto of current good things, the hub of the hub.

And it was the work of one man. Fields was the *genius
loci*. Fields, with his gentle spirit, his generous and ready
sympathy, his love of letters and of literary men, his fine
taste, his delightful humor, his business tact and skill,
drew, as a magnet draws its own, every kind of man, the
shy and the elusive as well as the gay men of the world
and the self-possessed favorites of the people. It was his
pride to have so many of the American worthies upon his
list of authors, to place there if he could the English poets
and "belles-lettres" writers, and then to call them all personal friends.

This passage from the sensitive pen of Curtis has more to do with Fields as a publisher of books, and as the human being he was in all his relations, than as editor of the *Atlantic*. It can fortunately be supplemented by some paragraphs from T. W. Higginson's "Cheerful Yesterdays," specifically dealing with Fields in his editorial capacity:—

In 1859 the *Atlantic Monthly* passed into the hands of Ticknor & Fields, the junior partner becoming finally its editor. It was a change of much importance to all its contributors, and greatly affected my own literary life. Lowell had been, of course, an appreciative and a sympathetic editor, yet sometimes dilatory and exasperating. Thus, a paper of mine on Theodore Parker, which should have appeared directly after the death of its subject, was delayed for five months by being accidentally put under a pile of unexamined manuscripts. Lowell had, moreover, some conservative reactions, and my essay "Ought Women to Learn the Alphabet?" which would now seem very innocent and probably had a wider circulation than any other magazine article I ever wrote, was not accepted without some shaking of the head, though it was finally given the place of honor in the number. Fields had the advantage over Lowell of being both editor and publisher, so that he had a free hand as to paying for articles. The prices then paid were lower than now, but were raised steadily; and he first introduced the practice of paying for each manuscript on acceptance, though he always lamented that this failed of its end so far as he was individually concerned. His object was to quiet the impatience of those whose contributions were delayed; but he declared that such persons complained more than ever, saying, "Since you valued my contribution so highly as to pay for it, you surely should print it at once." He had a virtue which I have never known in any other editor or publisher — that of

volunteering to advance money on prospective articles, yet
to be written; and he did this more than once to me. I
have also known him to increase the amount paid, on finding that an author particularly needed the money, especially if this were the case of a woman. His sympathy with
struggling women was always very great; and I think he
was the only one in the early *Atlantic* circle, except Whittier and myself, — with Emerson also, latterly, — who
favored woman suffrage. This financial kindliness was a
part of his general theory of establishing a staff, in which
effort he really succeeded, most of his contributors then
writing only for him — an aim which his successors abandoned, as doubtless became inevitable in view of the rapid
multiplication of magazines. Certainly there was something very pleasant about Fields's policy on this point;
and perhaps he petted us all rather too much. He had
some of the defects of his qualities — could not help being
a little of a flatterer, and sometimes, though not always,
evading the telling of wholesome truths.

I happened to be one of his favorites; he even wished
me, at one time, to undertake the whole critical department, which I luckily declined, although it appears by
the index that I wrote more largely for the first twenty
volumes of the magazine than any other contributor except Lowell and Holmes. Fields was constantly urging
me to attempt fiction, and when I somewhat reluctantly
followed his advice, he thought better of the result, I believe, than any one else did; for my story of "Malbone,"
especially, he prophesied a fame which the public has not
confirmed. Yet he was not indiscriminate in his praise,
and suggested some amendments which improved the tale
very much. He was capable also of being influenced by
argument, and was really the only editor I have ever en-
countered whose judgment I could move for an instant by
any cajoling; editors being, as a rule, a race of adamant,
as they should be. On the other hand, he advised strongly
against my writing the "Young Folks' History of the

EDWARD EVERETT HALE

whose " Man Without a Country " first appeared in the
Atlantic Monthly for December, 1863.

United States," which nevertheless turned out incomparably the most successful venture I ever made, having sold to the extent of two hundred thousand copies, and still selling well after twenty years. His practical judgment was thus not infallible, but it came nearer to it than that of any other literary man I have ever known. With all his desire to create a staff, Fields was always eagerly looking out for new talent, and was ever prompt to counsel and encourage.

Fields was the editor of the *Atlantic* throughout the Civil War; and it is interesting to note the part played by the magazine, under him, in the enlightenment and guidance of the public mind through that national crisis. From its very beginning, when Edmund Quincy contributed to the second issue his denunciation of slavery in an article, "Where Will It End?" so vehement in its tone that Norton wrote to Clough, "It is a new thing to see a magazine in this country take such ground" — even thus, before the war-cloud broke, there could have been no doubt where the *Atlantic* would stand upon the issues of the conflict. But as one turns over the pages of the volumes from 1861 to 1865, one is struck with the fact that, although the war is constantly reflected in them, this reflection does not usually appear in more than one or two items in the monthly programme. By far the greater portion of each issue was devoted to the fiction, the essays, the poetry, the criticism that would have appeared in any period of peace. A department in which the magazine most clearly sought to influence opinion was that of the political article, editorial in its character, for which Lowell and Parke Godwin had established so definite a precedent. Then there were the special papers, like Emerson's on "The President's Proclamation" (November, 1862), Holmes's "My Hunt for the Captain" (December, 1862), Hawthorne's "Chiefly about War Matters" (July, 1862), and Dr. Hale's national classic, the story of "The Man without a Country" (December, 1863).

Of Hawthorne's article just mentioned, it should be said in passing that the manner of its presentation speaks volumes for the strength of the friendship between Hawthorne and Fields: it was so underscored with foot-notes of editorial dissent, — together with statements that peculiarly objectionable passages had been omitted, — that a reader at the time might readily have imagined the breaking-off of all personal relations between author and editor. Donald G. Mitchell, indeed, wrote to Hawthorne when the article was printed: "I am glad to see your work in the *Atlantic,* but should be ready to swear at the marginal impertinences. Pray, is Governor Andrew editor? A man's opinions can take no catholic or philosophic range nowadays, but they call out some shrewish accusation of disloyalty." As a matter of fact, Fields and Hawthorne remained the closest of friends until Hawthorne's death, after which Fields, in his "Yesterdays with Authors," related the fact, not only that the changes, including the omissions of an unrestrained description of President Lincoln's personal appearance, were made with the author's good-natured consent, but that Hawthorne himself wrote all the foot-notes! The knowledge of this circumstance gives a special pungency of satisfaction to the note under the passage in which Hawthorne rejoiced at the hanging of John Brown: "Can it be a son of old Massachusetts who utters this abominable sentiment? For shame!"

To return to the other expressions of the spirit of

the time in the magazine, it was nowhere more dis-
cernible than in the poetry. Lowell's "Washers of the
Shroud," one of the most memorable of his poems on
national topics, appeared in the *Atlantic* of November,
1861. At the instance of Fields, he began, in January,
1862, his second series of "Biglow Papers," which continued intermittently until May, 1866. In September,
1865, his "Commemoration Ode" was printed in the
Atlantic. Whittier was represented during the four
dark years by many war-poems, including "Barbara
Frietchie." Longfellow's "Cumberland" appeared in
December, 1862; his "Killed at the Ford," in April,
1866. On the first page of the issue of February, 1862,
Mrs. Howe's "Battle Hymn of the Republic" first saw
the light. In October, 1863, came Emerson's "Voluntaries," — with its immediately and eternally provoca-
tive lines: —

> When Duty whispers low, *Thou must,*
> The youth replies, *I can.*

Such instances as these—and they might be greatly
multiplied—illustrate the fact that the pages of the
Atlantic were in large measure merely the medium for
the expression of what was uppermost in the minds of
its contributors. The appearance of the contributions
which have just been named was no more characteristic
of the magazine at the time than the fact that in the
Atlantic of June, 1864, Robert Browning gave the
world, in his "Prospice," one of his lyrics which the
world has most cherished. It may fairly be said that
the war, as a definite topic, did not receive the special
emphasis for which the periodical of a later day would
surely have made the passing events of such a crisis the
occasion. The clear inference is that the editors of

JULIA WARD HOWE
whose "Battle Hymn of the Republic" first appeared
in the *Atlantic Monthly* for February, 1862.

fifty years ago were far more likely than their successors of our own time to take what came to them, and
be thankful, — as well they might, — than to seek dili-
gently for contributions of a special nature. A reader
of the present-day *Atlantic* has called attention to the
fact that recently, wishing to inform himself about the
issues of the Franco-Prussian War, he sought for
some light upon the subject in the *Atlantics* of 1870 and
thereabouts — and sought in vain. In view of the brevity and concentration of that conflict, this is hardly
surprising. Yet this reader might have found in the
Atlantic of April, 1871, an article, by J. K. Hosmer,
on "The Giant in the Spiked Helmet," which is not
without its bearing even upon present circumstances.
Our own Spanish War, though not a world-shaking
circumstance, left a much clearer trace, in editorial
and special articles, in the *Atlantic* of 1898. But in
leaving the war of 1861–65 to take care, in considerable
measure, of itself, so to speak, Fields cannot be called
other than editor of his own time.

There was one episode of the period of his editorship
— though it happened to fall while he himself was in
Europe — which throws a significant light upon the
ways of the reading public in the sixties. This was the
publication, in the issue of September, 1869, of Mrs.
Stowe's article, "The True Story of Lady Byron's Life,"
an exceedingly outspoken "revelation" of Lord Byron's
personal character. It would be apart from the present purpose to recite the circumstances of its publication or the hideous charges it contained. What is note-
worthy, with special reference to the history of the
Atlantic, is that the article so outraged a large number of its readers that the circulation of the magazine
suffered a grievous reduction — indeed, so serious a blow

that the recovery from it was not accomplished for many years. Now that it has become ancient history, it may be calmly regarded as a conspicuous instance of the "Stop-the-Tribune" habit, through which the readers of an older generation tellingly registered their disapproval even of a favorite periodical. An editor of our own time might be wary of putting his clientèle to so stringent a test of adherence as this occasion provided; yet it may fairly be questioned whether even such an action as the *Atlantic's* in printing the Lady Byron article, backed as it was by the powerful prestige of Mrs. Stowe's signature, would now be visited so disastrously upon the offending magazine. This is really a large social question, involving the whole temper of the reading public and its past and present capacity for expressing its own moral indignation. If the edge of the older capacity is dulled, who shall say that we are better off?

As the editorship of Fields bore so close a relation to the *Atlantic's* change of ownership, there will perhaps be no more fitting occasion than at this point to record the succession of publishing firms which have been responsible for the magazine. Only three volumes, beginning November, 1857, and ending June, 1859, were published by Phillips, Sampson & Co., at 13 Winter Street, Boston. Volumes IV to XXI, inclusive (July, 1859, to June, 1868), bore the imprint of Ticknor & Fields, whose office, through Volume XV (ending June, 1865), was at 135 Washington Street, — the Old Corner Bookstore, — and thereafter at 124 Tremont Street, opposite the Park Street Church. Volumes XXII to XXVI (July, 1868, to December, 1870), inclusive, were issued by Fields, Osgood & Co., who defined themselves as "Successors to Ticknor & Fields." From volume

XXVII to XXXII (January, 1871, to December, 1873),
the imprint was that of James R. Osgood & Co., "Late
Ticknor & Fields, and Fields, Osgood & Co." Then,
from January, 1874, to December, 1877 (volumes
XXXIII to XL), came the double imprint of "Boston:
H. O. Houghton & Co., New York: Hurd & Houghton."
The four following volumes, XLI–XLIV (January,
1878, to December, 1879), were published by Houghton,
Osgood & Co. In January, 1880 (volume XLV), began
the long ownership of Houghton, Mifflin and Company,
which continued through the first number of volume
CII (July, 1908). Since then the magazine has been
published by the Atlantic Monthly Company.

Through all these changes, which have come naturally and without distressing transitions, the home of
the *Atlantic* has almost invariably been an agreeable
place; even if it were possible to visualize it under
every editor and publisher, space for such a process
would here be inadequate. Fortunately, however, this
can be done for the period of Fields's control, through
reproducing most of a paper, "The *Atlantic's* Pleasant
Days in Tremont Street," which appeared unsigned
in the *Atlantic* of November, 1907, and was written
by Miss Susan M. Francis, an editorial assistant of
every *Atlantic* editor except only the first and the
eighth. Her picture of Fields himself supplements ex-
cellently what has already been related of him.

My first knowledge of the making of the *Atlantic* was
in the last years of Mr. Fields's editorship and of his connection with the house of Ticknor and Fields, or, as it
was at his retirement, Fields, Osgood and Co. The office
was his private room at 124 Tremont Street, one of the
spacious dwelling-houses, of an earlier generation, in that
street, which business had of a sudden absorbed and in

some sort reconstructed. His was the smaller front room on the second floor, — the larger, in which Mr. Aldrich, as editor of "Every Saturday," had his desk, was a general reception-room, — with one window looking upon Tremont Street, and another upon Hamilton Place. It was a cheerful little room, with open fire, opposite to which was a sofa for visitors, with prints, mostly portraits, upon the walls, and Mr. Fields's standing desk in one corner, on which lay an always open book in which from time to time he noted appointments of all sorts, and every other thing, no matter how trifling, that he wished to remember, the recent pages being always carefully examined more than once a day. This habit, among others, made him one of the most dependable persons I have ever known. He never forgot an engagement of any kind or the slightest promise and he was punctuality itself. . . . The broad window seats were covered with MSS., while on the floor were piled books sent to the magazine. Mr. Howells, the assistant editor, did his work, the greater part of the actual editorial labor, at his home in Cambridge or at the University Press. Mr. Fields was at that time unable to use his hand in writing, and dictated his letters, beside requiring other assistance. Between whiles, I was set to weed out the MSS., so that the hopeless need not be sent to Cambridge. Typewriters had not come, to save editorial eyes, and, to my inexperience, a large part of the effusions were at first more or less illegible, while the number written with pale ink on thin paper and rolled seemed painfully large. When I kept an exact account in later times, the number of MSS. received from year to year hardly varied, and I should judge that it was much the same in those days, for if there were fewer writers, there were fewer magazines. The volume of stories was large, but the "dialect story," so-called, was then inconspicuous, and chiefly represented by New England rural tales and fishing-village sketches. The wild west was hardly in evidence, and there were not many war stories. It was too near to write easily of — what there were usually came from Northern pens. There were certainly as many verses as to-day, with the same tendency toward a widespread outburst of rhyme on any sensation of the hour.

THE SCENE OF THE "ATLANTIC'S PLEASANT
DAYS IN TREMONT STREET"

But it is impossible to say much about that room without speaking particularly of Mr. Fields, the gracious host of more distinguished visitors than any other *Atlantic* office can have known. Like all men who have risen to an enviable position without extraneous aid of any sort, Mr. Fields had detractors and unfriends who were willing to magnify any little foible or affectation; but I, — and I only speak of myself by way of illustration, — coming to him very young and self-distrustful, suddenly faced with the problem of earning a living, and fully conscious of no training for that end, shall be thankful and grateful to the last day of my life, that at the outset I fell into such kind, considerate hands. I knew that I often did badly, I know it better now; but there was never a word of blame or even a look of annoyance, while for anything that could by any possibility be commended, praise was never lacking. Always there was thoughtful courtesy and a pleasant humor, making dull tasks easy. No one could have been gentler or more sympathetic to the procession of literary aspirants who found their way to him, though he firmly refused to be bored beyond reasonable limits, and seemed to have discovered the secret of the inclined plane for lingering visitors which Dr. Holmes longed for, the inclination as imperceptible to most as it was efficacious. Love of literature was as genuine and heart-felt a feeling in him as in any one I have ever known. Not a writer, — in any literary sense, — he had an unbounded and generous appreciation of the literary gifts of others, and was even willing, not once or twice, to publish to his own loss that which he felt was good. And it should be said that his judgment as to the commercial success of any venture was usually excellent, so far as one can judge in such matters, and that he was a very shrewd and competent man of business, one not in the least likely to be imposed upon or self-deceived in a question of affairs. I remember his speaking to me in those days and later of the deterioration in the taste of American readers which he believed had set in after the war. Before, he declared, any good edition of a good book was almost sure of at least a fair sale — a surety which seemed to have quite passed away. There were many more readers, but the best books were less read.

As I look back on those few years, nothing impresses me so much as the good spirits, even the gayety, that pervaded the establishment. I think it was a very prosperous time for the *Atlantic,* loyally supported as it was by the best writers in the country, and with practically hardly a rival in its own kind; while business flourished amain. . . . The members of the house, Mr. Aldrich, Mr. Anthony (the art manager), Mr. Howells, when in town, and frequent guests, used to have luncheon every day (brought in from the Parker House, I think) in an upstairs room. This must have been a particularly cheerful board — certainly those who sat round it could make it so. As for the visitors in Mr. Fields's little room, I remember one day when Emerson, Longfellow, Lowell, Holmes, and Whittier were all crowded together there, when the portly figure of Mr. Bayard Taylor blocked the doorway, and it was decided to seek seats and space in a larger room. Visitors such as these need not be described — that has been done so often and sometimes so well, that I could scarcely presume to give my superficial and superfluous impressions, though I can say that for brilliant, suggestive, entertaining, pungent, and humorous talk, no one of them, not even Dr. Holmes, nor any other man of letters whom I have met, could be compared to Lowell. . . .

As I recall those pleasant rooms in Tremont Street, it seems as though they were always full of sunshine (they really had a northern exposure), as if the cheerfulness that pervaded them had left a visible brightness in the memory. There could not be grayness or dullness with Mr. Fields, Mr. Aldrich, and Mr. Osgood in possession, and the constant visitor, who, the chances were, would be wise, or witty, or both. Literary bores and cranks of course found their way there in considerable numbers, but they only appeared to give the needed relief. And much work was done, but nimbleness of spirit seemed to give quickness and deftness to head and hand. I think clouds and rain began to come when Mr. Fields retired. Perhaps he took from the house, besides more material things, a desirable element of conservatism and wise cau-

A corner in the library of James T. Fields in his Charles Street house,
for many years the centre of hospitality to the *Atlantic* circle ;
here also Dickens, Thackeray, and other English
visitors were familiar guests.

tion. For six months thereafter he retained the headship
of the magazine, when Mr. Howells became sole editor,
and there was no longer a Boston office. Mr. Fields still
retained his room, though he was in it less, and it was
still a resort for friends old and new. But there was a
change in the atmosphere of the establishment — new enterprises proved costly, and necessarily, at their outset,
unremunerative, and possibly times were changing everywhere. Then came the calamity of the Great Fire. The
Atlantic Monthly was sold to Messrs. Hurd and Houghton,
and, until that house united with that of J. R. Osgood
and Co., I knew nothing save by hearsay of the making of
the magazine. . . .

From the pleasant quarters in Tremont Street the house
moved to Winthrop Square, and never again till it reached
Park Street did it know the comforts of home, so to speak
— it had only business offices. The whole quarter of the
city where the new building stood was in a chaotic state —
rising from its ashes would, I suppose, be the proper expression. At that time came the consolidation of J. R.
Osgood and Co. with Hurd and Houghton, of course bring-
ing back the *Atlantic* and some of my old work therein.
But there was no real *Atlantic* office in that building,
which one winter night was burned to the ground. Many
Atlantic MSS. were burned with it — how many I never
exactly knew, for the book where they were recorded went
too. So far as I could recollect them, I wrote to the possible contributors of their loss; and as I remember, with
very few exceptions, they behaved exceedingly well, though
very few of them seemed to have kept copies, even of poems.

It was with a new name, Houghton, Mifflin and Co., that
the house came to Park Street. Here Mr. Howells on his
weekly visits had the use of a small, dark room, which
was certainly never considered an *Atlantic* office. That
came with Mr. Aldrich's assumption of the editorship, the
first office of the magazine in Boston since the Tremont
Street days.

In one of the foregoing paragraphs allusion has been
made to the "detractors and unfriends who were willing
to magnify any little foible or affectation" in Fields. Besides these, there was one contributor, Gail Hamilton,
who so completely "fell out" with him in matters of
business dealing — royalties, percentages, etc. — as to
make the publisher-editor of the *Atlantic* the chief subject of her satiric volume, "A Battle of the Books."
From its pages it is worth while to transcribe a passage reflecting a feeling which may not have been confined to a single recalcitrant. Its reading to-day may
possess some of the interest of the " Game of Authors."

There are never wanting persons who, not content with
writing history as it is, are always conjuring up what
would have been if things had happened differently. If
Charles I. had not lost his head, if Napoleon had beaten
at Waterloo, if Booth's pistol had missed fire, events
would have gone thus and thus. A fruitful field opens before such speculators in the history of our country's literature. Had Messrs. Brummell and Hunt gone into the
grocery business, for instance, Homer would have been
cobbling shoes at Haverhill, or at most, chronicling small
beer in a country newspaper. Dante would have been a
lawyer in chambers, drawing up wills and plodding
through deeds, but leaving no foot-prints on the sands of
time. Boccaccio would have been milking cows at Brook
Farm, or growing round-shouldered over his desk in the
Jerusalem Court House. Miriam would have been writing
stories for the "Little Cormorant," at fifty cents a column,
and as "Uncle Tom's Cabin" would never have been built,
the South would never have been provoked into rebellion;
we should have had no war and no greenbacks, prices
would never have risen, ten per cent. and fifteen cents
would have been the same, and we should all have died
comfortably in our beds.

There was a kindred note of complaint against the *Atlantic* circle of the day in an article, "Old Connecticut *vs.* the *Atlantic Monthly*," published in the April, 1865, issue of the New Haven quarterly, *The New Englander*. The author of this article, the Reverend Increase N. Tarbox, welcomed a flavor of "fresh talent from the outside world" in Donald G. Mitchell's story, "Dr. Johns," which began with 1865, and, on reading with joy an article in the *Atlantic* of February, 1865, on "The Pleiades of Connecticut," exclaimed: "We have often wished that a little of that conceit which centres about the city of Boston might be abated. Proud as she may well be of her position, we think she would stand in a more grand and noble attitude, if she had a juster conception of what has been and is going on elsewhere, and from what sources she herself derives no small share of her strength."

Whatever justice may have lain at the root of this feeling, it is a significant fact that in 1866, only one year later, a young Ohioan, William Dean Howells, recently returned from his consulship in Venice, became assistant editor of the *Atlantic*, and in 1871, on the retirement of Fields from the editorship, succeeded to his post.

WILLIAM DEAN HOWELLS
Third Editor of the *Atlantic Monthly*
1871-1881

III

It is a piece of complete good fortune that Mr. Howells himself, in his delightful volume, "Literary Friends and Acquaintance," in his "Recollections of an Atlantic Editorship," in the November, 1907, *Atlantic*, and elsewhere ("There are now so many other places!" he himself exclaimed in the *Atlantic* article), has made his association with the magazine a matter of such illuminating record. Even so early as in the editorship of Lowell, his first connection with the *Atlantic* was established through the acceptance and publication of several poems. This fact emboldened the youthful poet and journalist, on his first pilgrimage from Columbus to New England, in the summer of 1860, to present himself, timorously enough, to Lowell in Cambridge. The older man received him with the greatest friendliness and asked him to dine at the Parker House in Boston a few days later. Of the meeting there, a few of Mr. Howells's own paragraphs about it will give the best report.

As it fell out, I lived without further difficulty to the day and hour of the dinner Lowell made for me; and I really think, looking at myself impersonally, and remembering the sort of young fellow I was, that it would have been a great pity if I had not. The dinner was at the old-fashioned Boston hour of two, and the table was laid for four people in some little upper room at Parker's, which I was never afterwards able to make sure of. Lowell was already there when I came, and he presented me, to my inexpressible delight and surprise, to Dr. Holmes, who was there with him. . . .

A little while after, Fields came in, and then our number and my pleasure were complete.

Nothing else so richly satisfactory, indeed, as the whole affair could have happened to a like youth at such a point in his career; and when I sat down, with Doctor Holmes and Mr. Fields, on Lowell's right, I felt through and through the dramatic perfection of the event. The kindly Autocrat recognized some such quality of it in terms which were not the less precious and gracious for their humorous excess. I have no reason to think that he had yet read any of my poor verses, or had me otherwise than wholly on trust from Lowell; but he leaned over towards his host, and said, with a laughing look at me, "Well, James, this is something like the apostolic succession; this is the laying on of hands." I took his sweet and caressing irony as he meant it; but the charm of it went to my head long before any drop of wine, together with the charm of hearing him and Lowell calling each other James and Wendell, and of finding them still cordially boys together.

It was, indeed, far more than Holmes could possibly have foreseen, a laying on of hands, for two of Lowell's three guests were to follow him in the bishopric of the magazine, of which the third was to remain its coadjutor for life. The talk that made that dinner-table so memorable to Mr. Howells is devoutly recorded in his pages — also Lowell's promise of a letter of introduction to Hawthorne. The note that accompanied it is given in Lowell's "Letters," and bears its own testimony to the first editor's faith in his young contributor : —

CAMBRIDGE, *Monday*, *August*, 1860.

MY DEAR YOUNG FRIEND,—Here is a note to Mr. Hawthorne, which you can use if you have occasion.

Don't print too much and too soon; don't get married

in a hurry; read what will make you *think,* not *dream;* hold yourself dear, and more power to your elbow! God bless you!

Cordially yours,

J. R. LOWELL.

There was a reaffirmation of Lowell's confidence in his younger successor, when he wrote to Fields about an article by Mr. Howells in the January, 1869, *Atlantic:* "That boy will know how to write if he goes on, and then we old fellows will have to look about us."

Fields must have shared Lowell's immediate belief in Mr. Howells, for besides asking him to his own hospitable breakfast-table on the morning after the dinner at the Parker House, he imparted to the young man such a sense of friendliness that Mr. Howells went direct to him after his day in Concord and confided the discomfiture he had experienced in a visit to Emerson. Somehow he had felt himself sadly to blame for making so scant a success of his call upon Emerson, of which he wrote: —

By this time I could see it in a humorous light, and I did not much mind his lying back in his chair and laughing and laughing, till I thought he would roll out of it. He perfectly conceived the situation, and got an amusement from it that I could get only through sympathy with him. But I thought it a favorable moment to propose myself as the assistant editor of the *Atlantic Monthly* [Fields was then its publisher, not yet its editor], which I had the belief I could very well become, with advantage to myself, if not to the magazine. He seemed to think so too; he said that if the place had not just been filled, I should certainly have had it; and it was to his recollection of this prompt ambition of mine that I suppose I may have owed my succession to a like vacancy some four years later.

During this intervening period Mr. Howells had served his consulship in Venice, — from which resulted his early book "Venetian Days," — had returned to America, and settled in New York as a writer for the *Nation*. One evening in the winter of 1866 he met Mr. and Mrs. Fields at the house of Bayard Taylor. "Don't despise Boston!" Fields said to him; and he replied, "Few are worthy to live in Boston." Three days later he received a letter from Fields asking him to become assistant editor of the *Atlantic*. After some consideration of the offer, says Mr. Howells, —

I went to Boston to see Mr. Fields concerning details. I was to sift all the manuscripts and correspond with contributors; I was to do the literary proof-reading of the magazine; and I was to write the four or five pages of book-notices, which were then printed at the end of the periodical in finer type; and I was to have forty dollars a week. I said that I was getting that already for less work, and then Mr. Fields offered me ten dollars more. Upon these terms we closed, and on the 1st of March, which was my twenty-ninth birthday, I went to Boston and began my work. I had not decided to accept the place without advising with Lowell; he counselled the step, and gave me some shrewd and useful suggestions. The whole affair was conducted by Fields with his unfailing tact and kindness, but it could not be kept from me that the qualification I had as a practical printer for the work was most valued, and that as proof-reader I was expected to make it avail on the side of economy. Somewhere in life's feast the course of humble-pie must always come in; and if I did not wholly relish this bit of it, I dare say it was good for me, and I digested it perfectly.

The extent and value of Mr. Howells's work for the *Atlantic* for fifteen years, first as assistant editor, then for about ten years as editor, can hardly be estimated. His own modest and charming story of it all is to be found in the book and magazine article already mentioned. To illustrate the more technical side of his labors, a paragraph may be taken from his "Recollections of an Atlantic Editorship":—

Except for the brief period of a year or eighteen months, I had no assistance during my editorship. During the greater part of the time I had clerkly help, most efficient, most intelligent; but I read all the manuscripts which claimed critical attention; I wrote to contributors who merited more than a printed circular; I revised all the proofs, verifying every quotation and foreign word, and correcting slovenly style and syntax, and then I revised the author's and my own corrections. Meanwhile I was writing, not only criticisms, but sketches, stories, and poems for the body of the magazine; and in the course of time, a novel each year. It seems like rather full work, but I had always leisure, and I made a long summer away from Cambridge in the country. The secret, if there was any secret, lay in my doing every day two or three hours' work, and letting no day pass idly. The work of reading manuscripts and writing letters could be pushed into a corner, and taken out for some interval of larger leisure; and this happened oftener and oftener as I grew more and more a novelist, and needed every morning for fiction. The proof-reading, which was seldom other than a pleasure, with the tasks of revision and research, I kept for the later afternoons and evenings; though sometimes it took well-nigh the character of original work, in that liberal *Atlantic* tradition of bettering the authors by editorial transposition and paraphrase, either in the form of suggestion or of absolute correction. This proof-read-

ing was a school of verbal exactness and rhetorical sim-
plicity and clearness, and in it I had succeeded others,
my superiors, who were without their equals. It is still
my belief that the best proof-reading in the world is done
in Cambridge, Massachusetts, and it is probably none
the worse for my having a part in it no longer.

As I have intimated, I found it by no means drudgery;
though as for drudgery, I think that this is for the most
part in the doer of it, and it always is a very wholesome
thing, even when it is real, objective drudgery. It would
be a much decenter, honester, and juster world if we each
took his share in it, and I base my best hopes of the future
in some such eventuality. Not only the proofs were a
pleasant and profitable drudgery, but the poor manuscripts, except in the most forbidding and hopeless instances, yielded their little crumbs of comfort; they supported while they fatigued.

Such were the details of Mr. Howells's laborious
days. The spirit in which all his work was done — the
essential kindliness of all its human relationships, the
constant hospitality to new ideas and new writers,
everything that an eager mind and a generous personality could contribute to the functions of an editor —
shines through the record of his *Atlantic* years. To
his special credit must be counted the lengthening of
its tent-ropes. "The fact is," he says, "we were growing, whether we liked it or not, more and more American. Without ceasing to be New England, without ceasing to be Bostonian at heart, we had become southern,
mid-western, and far-western in our sympathies. It
seemed to me that the new good things were coming
from those regions rather than from our own coasts and
hills, but it may have been that the things were newer
oftener than better." Thus it was characteristic of

him to have suggested to Mark Twain his writing for
the *Atlantic* his "Old Times on the Mississippi"—or
perhaps rather to have recorded the circumstance by
saying, "I hope I am not too fondly mistaken in thinking I suggested his writing [it] for the magazine." Of
Mark Twain's very first contribution to the *Atlantic,*
he says: "'A True Story' was but three pages long,
and I remember the anxiety with which the business
side of the magazine tried to compute its pecuniary
value. It was finally decided to give the author twenty
dollars a page, a rate unexampled in our modest history. I believe Mr. Clemens has since been offered a
thousand dollars a thousand words, but I have never
regretted that we paid him so handsomely for his first
contribution."

At the invitation of Fields, prompted by Miss Francis, Bret Harte had first written for the *Atlantic.* It
was with Howells, in Cambridge, that he made his stay
when, several years later, in 1871, he made his tri-
umphal progress to the East. Then it was, according
to Mr. Henry C. Merwin's "Life of Bret Harte," that
the New York publishers made him inadequate offers
for his writings, "and a few days later Bret Harte accepted the offer of James R. Osgood and Company, then
publishers of the *Atlantic,* to pay him ten thousand
dollars during the ensuing year for whatever he might
write in the twelve months, be it much or little. This
offer, a magnificent one for the time, was made despite
the astonishing fact that of the first volume of Bret
Harte's stories, issued by the same publishers six
months before, only thirty-five hundred copies had then
been sold." Harte redeemed the arrangement by con-
tributing to the *Atlantic* four stories, one of which
was "How Santa Claus Came to Simpson's Bar," and

five poems. It is easy to detect the hand of Mr. Howells
in the whole transaction.

The older writers of the New England group remained faithful to the *Atlantic* — even Whittier, after
Mr. Howells, in what he afterwards felt to be a mistaken exercise of his editorial authority, had declined
one of his poems. To the promising members of the
younger group Mr. Howells's welcome was unfailingly
cordial—to none more so than to the fellow novelist and
contemporary, Henry James, with whose work his own
was so often compared and contrasted. "My desert in
valuing him," says Mr. Howells, "is so great that I can
confess the fact that two of his stories and one of his
criticisms appeared in the magazine some years before
my time, though perhaps not with the band of music
with which I welcomed every one afterwards." Giving
full credit also to his predecessor for the recognition
of the quality in the stories of Miss Sarah Orne Jewett,
he adds: "It is the foible of editors, if it is not
rather their forte, to flatter themselves that, though
they may not have invented their contributions, they
have at least invented their contributors; and if any
long-memoried reader chooses to hail me as an inspired
genius because of my instant and constant appreciation
of Miss Jewett's writing, I shall be the last to snub
him down."

Another of the feminine contributors to the *Atlantic,*
though not immediately accredited to this company,
received prompt recognition from Mr. Howells, who
shall tell the story himself : —

I do not remember any man who feigned himself a
woman, but now and then a woman liked to masquerade
as a man, though the disguise never deceived the editor,

even when it deceived the reader, except in the very signal and very noted instance of Miss Mary N. Murfree, whom, till I met her face to face, I never suspected for any but Charles Egbert Craddock. The severely simple, the robust, the athletic hand which she wrote would have sufficed to carry conviction of her manhood against any doubts. I believe I took the first story she sent, and for three or four years I addressed my letters of acceptance, or criticism, to Charles Egbert Craddock, Murfreesboro, Tennessee, without the slightest misgiving. Then she came to Boston, and Aldrich, who had succeeded me, and who had already suffered the disillusion awaiting me, asked me to meet Craddock at dinner. He had asked Dr. Holmes and Lawrence Barrett, too; and I should not attempt to say whose astonishment he enjoyed most. But I wish I could recall word for word the exquisite terms in which Dr. Holmes turned his discomfiture into triumph, in that most delicately feminine presence.

Still another Boston editor of the same period — it may be said without digressing too widely — fell into still more serious trouble through the Southern practice of not restricting masculine names to men. This irreproachable bachelor had long been in correspondence with another Tennessee writer whom he had assumed to be of his own sex, and hearing that "he" was coming to Boston at a certain time wrote a cordial letter inviting "him" to share his room in the boarding-house of his long inhabitance. To his utter discomfiture a Southern lady announced herself one day in his office as the recipient of his invitation. It is not reported that any Dr. Holmes was at hand to save the situation with his verbal agility.

If the experience of Mr. Howells with Miss Murfree was unique in *Atlantic* annals, it was not the only

novelty connected with his editorship. One innovation
of his own he described in writing. "For a while, I
think for a year, I indulged the fancy of printing each
month a piece of original music, with original songs;
but though both the music and the songs were good,
or at least from our best younger composers and poets,
the feature did not please — I do not know why — and
it was presently omitted."

In the unadorned pages of the *Atlantic* these songs to-
day present a somewhat strange appearance; but there
they are — Whittier's "Hymn written for the Opening
of the International Exhibition, Philadelphia, May 10,
1876," with its music by John K. Paine, filling together
two pages in June, 1876; and later, the "Sunset Song"
of Celia Thaxter and Julius Eichberg, the "Creole
Lover's Song" of Edmund C. Stedman and Dudley
Buck, "A Dream" by W. W. Story and F. Boott, a
"Song" by George Parsons Lathrop and George L. Osgood. There were also many bits of musical score in
the papers of musical criticism which William F. Apthorp long contributed to the magazine. Excellent
line drawings, moreover, accompanied the series of
articles on "Crude and Curious Inventions at the Cen-
tennial Exhibition," by Edward H. Knight. In the
previous decades of the sixties many simple sketches
had illustrated Agassiz's articles on various processes
of nature. A paper on "The New Gymnastics" by Dr.
Dio Lewis, in the issue of August, 1862, — a physical-
culture article which would now be thought more ap-
propriate to a Sunday newspaper, — carried with it
forty-three remarkably inartistic drawings of men and
women exercising with dumb-bells, rings, wands, and
bean-bags. Thus the *Atlantic*, which, in spite of its
occasional necessary maps, diagrams, and the like, has

never been one of the illustrated periodicals, has had its moments of pictorial adornment — and Mr. Howells's introduction of pages not wholly given to reading-matter was not, after all, a complete innovation.

THE TICKNOR MANSION
at the head of Park Street.

One portion of the magazine — a department now sufficiently venerable — owed its origin entirely to him. This is the "Contributors' Club," of which he has written: —

In the course of time, but a very long time, the magazine felt the need of a more informal expression than it found in the stated articles, and the Contributors' Club took the place of all the different departments, those of politics, music, and art having been dropped before that of literature. The new idea was talked over with the late George

Parsons Lathrop, who had become my assistant, and we found no way to realize it but by writing the first paragraphs ourselves, and so tempting others to write for the Club. In the course of a very few months we had more than help enough, and could easily drop out of the co-operation.

During the period of Mr. Howells's editorship one practice of an earlier day was revived — that of the meeting together of editors, publishers, and contributors at the dinner-table. Several occasions of this nature are described in Arthur Gilman's article, "Atlantic Dinners and Diners," in the Fiftieth Anniversary number of the magazine. The first of these revivals of a past custom took place at the Parker House, December 15, 1874, and marked the acquisition of the magazine by the firm of H. O. Houghton & Co. On Whittier's seventieth birthday, December 17, 1877, another notable assembling of the masculine pillars of the *Atlantic,* as guests of its publishers, occurred at the Brunswick Hotel in Boston; still another, at the same place, on December 3, 1879, in celebration of Dr. Holmes's seventieth birthday, which had fallen inconveniently on the 29th of the previous August. "When the day arrived," wrote Mr. Gilman, "more than one hundred sat together around six large tables. A remarkable change is found in the fact that more than one-third of the company were ladies!" The next, and last, festivity of the kind was itself in honor of a lady, Harriet Beecher Stowe, and marked her seventy-first birthday, June 14, 1882, by which time Aldrich had succeeded Mr. Howells in the editorship of the magazine. It took the form of an out-door luncheon on the grounds of Governor Claflin at Newtonville.

At each of these feasts the towering figures of New England letters — it is superfluous to catalogue them — were present, and speeches and verses of all possible fitness, grace, and feeling were uttered. When the un-expected happens, it is often more illuminating than the expected. Let us therefore pass over all the felici-tous expressions at the gatherings of what so nearly resembled a clan, and draw perhaps a truer impression of the general scene from Mr. Howells's own account, in his "My Mark Twain," of the havoc wrought by the great humorist on the occasion of the dinner in honor of Whittier.

The passing years have left me in the dark as to the pretext of that supper at which Clemens made his awful speech, and came so near being the death of us all. At the breakfasts and luncheons we had the pleasure of our lady contributors' company, but that night there were only men, and because of our great strength we survived.

I suppose the year was about 1879, but here the almanac is unimportant, and I can only say that it was after Clemens had become a very valued contributor of the magazine, where he found himself to his own great explicit satisfaction. He had jubilantly accepted our invitation, and had promised a speech, which it appeared afterwards he had prepared with unusual care and confidence. He believed he had been particularly fortunate in his notion for the speech of that evening, and he had worked it out in joyous self-reliance. It was the notion of three tramps, three dead-beats, visiting a California mining-camp, and imposing themselves upon the innocent miners as respec-tively Ralph Waldo Emerson, Henry Wadsworth Long-fellow, and Oliver Wendell Holmes. The humor of the conception must prosper or fail according to the mood of the hearer, but Clemens felt sure of compelling this to sympathy, and he looked forward to an unparalleled triumph.

But there were two things that he had not taken into account. One was the species of religious veneration in which these men were held by those nearest them, a thing that I should not be able to realize to people remote from them in time and place. They were men of extraordinary dignity, of the thing called *presence,* for want of some clearer word, so that no one could well approach them in a light or trifling spirit. I do not suppose that anybody more truly valued them or more piously loved them than Clemens himself, but the intoxication of his fancy carried them beyond the bounds of that regard, and emboldened him to the other thing which he had not taken into account — namely, the immense hazard of working his fancy out before their faces, and expecting them to enter into the delight of it. If neither Emerson, nor Longfellow, nor Holmes had been there, the scheme might possibly have carried; but even this is doubtful, for those who so devoutly honored them would have overcome their horror with difficulty, and perhaps would not have overcome it at all.

The publisher, with a modesty very ungrateful to me, had abdicated his office of host, and I was the hapless president, fulfilling the abhorred function of calling people to their feet and making them speak. When I came to Clemens, I introduced him with the cordial admiring I had for him as one of my greatest contributors and dearest friends. Here, I said, in sum, was a humorist who never left you hanging your head for having enjoyed his joke; and then the amazing mistake, the bewildering blunder, the cruel catastrophe was upon us. I believe that, after the scope of the burlesque made itself clear, there was no one there, including the burlesquer himself, who was not smitten with a desolating dismay. There fell a silence, weighing many tons to the square inch, which deepened from moment to moment, and was broken only by the hysterical and blood-curdling laughter of a single guest, whose name shall not be handed down to infamy. Nobody knew whether to look at the speaker or down at his plate. I chose my plate as the least affliction, and so I do not know how Clemens looked, except when I stole a glance at him, and saw him standing solitary among his appalled and appalling listeners, with his joke dead on his hands. From a first glance at the great three whom his jest had made its theme, I was aware of Longfellow sitting upright, and regarding the humorist with an air of pensive puzzle, of Holmes busily writing on his menu, with a well-feigned effect of preoccupation, and of Emerson holding his elbows, and listening with a sort of Jovian oblivion of this nether world in that lapse of memory which saved him in those later years from so much bother. Clemens must have dragged his joke to the climax and left it there, but I cannot say this from any sense of the fact. Of what happened afterward at the table where the immense, the wholly innocent, the truly unimagined affront was offered, I have no longer the least remembrance. I next remember being in a room of the hotel, where Clemens was not to sleep, but to toss in despair, and Charles Dudley Warner's saying, in the gloom, " Well, Mark *you're* a funny fellow." It was as well as anything else he could have said, but Clemens seemed unable to accept the tribute.

So wretched, indeed, was Mark Twain over the whole performance that on his return to Hartford, he wrote to Mr. Howells: "It will hurt the *Atlantic* for me to appear in its pages now"; and begged his friend to return the proofs of a story then awaiting publication.

A humor so genuine as that which Mr. Howells reveals in his account of " the cruel catastrophe " is needed to cope, not only with a humorist, but with the daily transactions of life. His whole mental and spiritual attitude, as it appears in his own retrospect of his editorship of the *Atlantic,* constituted an ideal element of qualification for his task. No other editor, assistant and chief, has been associated with the magazine for so many years as the fifteen which Mr. Howells gave to this work. It could not have been otherwise than that his labors should have continued long to yield their fruits. "The magazine," he has himself written, "was already established in its traditions when I came to it, and when I left it fifteen years later, it seemed to me that if I had done any good, it was little more than to fix it more firmly in them." "Little more" are the words in this sentence which another hand would especially revise.

IV

The ensuing seventeen years, 1881–1898, were divided in the *Atlantic* editorship, between two men, Thomas Bailey Aldrich and Horace Elisha Scudder, of whom Aldrich held the post for nine, Scudder for eight years. These were the two editors of a later day who have been first to follow Lowell and Fields beyond the sight of the present generation. Each stepped naturally into the editorial office, and each brought with him and gave to the magazine something distinctive and valuable.

There are two incidents linking Aldrich characteristically with the first two editors of the *Atlantic* wholly in their editorial capacity. In Mr. Ferris Greenslet's " Life of Thomas Bailey Aldrich " it is related that for the first three years of the *Atlantic's* existence, he had offered poetical contributions, without success. (Elsewhere it appears that in the pride of his youth, he had lost one opportunity to appear in the *Atlantic* through not changing a faulty rhyme in one of his poems, which he subsequently mended.) At length, in April of 1860, he received the following note from Lowell: —

My dear Sir,—

I welcome you heartily to the *Atlantic*. When I receive so fine a poem as "Pythagoras," I don't think the check of Messrs. Ticknor & Fields pays for it. I must add some thanks and appreciation. I have put it down for June.

Very truly yours,

J. R. Lowell.

THOMAS BAILEY ALDRICH
Fourth Editor of the *Atlantic Monthly*
1881–1890

The true flavor of Aldrich was imparted to the incident long afterwards. "Twenty-five years later," says Mr. Greenslet, "when Aldrich in his turn had become editor of the *Atlantic*, he accepted a poem that Lowell sent him, with a copy of this note. Lowell promptly called at the office to say that he was so enheartened by its recognition that he had about made up his mind to follow literature as a profession."

His early contact with Fields as editor was even more characteristic. The story goes that, bearing a poem of his own one day to Fields's office in the Old Corner Bookstore, he found the editor out, but noticed on his desk a memorandum of things to be done at once. "Don't forget to mail E—— his contract," he read; and "Don't forget H——'s proof." With a delicious impudence the young poet wrote beneath these reminders of obligations to Emerson and Holmes, "Don't forget to accept A——'s poem," left the manuscript, and departed. "The poem" — as Professor Bliss Perry repeats the anecdote in his "Park Street Papers" — "was accepted, paid for, and, truest kindness of all, — as Mr. Aldrich asserted, — was never printed. But the resourceful youth never lost his deferential attitude toward the bearers of those famous initialed names that had once preceded his own."

It has been said that Aldrich stepped naturally into the *Atlantic* editorship. When Howells came from New York to Boston, in 1868, as assistant editor of the magazine, he found Aldrich installed, but a few months earlier, in the office of the same publishing house, as editor of its weekly journal, *Every Saturday.* Aldrich had already gained a considerable editorial experience in New York, in connection with several periodicals, the suspension of one of which, the *Saturday Press,* he had announced in terms bearing his distinctive touch: "This paper is discontinued for lack of funds, which is, by a coincidence, precisely the reason for which it was started." Of the Aldrich that Mr. Howells found in Boston he has written: "We were of nearly the same age, but he had a distinct and distinguished priority of reputation, in so much that in my Western remoteness I had always ranged him with such elders and betters of mine as Holmes and Lowell, and never imagined him the blonde, slight youth I found him, with every imaginable charm of contemporaneity."

The two young men became the best of friends, and in their other friendships none should more surely be counted than those they formed with their employers, Fields, and his younger partner, James R. Osgood. On the retirement of Fields from the firm, Osgood, whose "reach," as Mr. Greenslet has well put it, "rather exceeded his grasp," undertook expansion which led to business disaster. When the *Atlantic* was sold to H. O. Houghton & Co., *Every Saturday,* also disposed of, was suppressed. Mr. Howells records some sort of funereal rite in which he and Aldrich joined with Osgood, on the day after the sale, and the spirit in which the three men had worked together reveals itself clearly in his words about Osgood:—

We all knew that it was his necessity that had caused him to part with the periodicals; but he professed that it was his pleasure, and he said, He had not felt so light-hearted since he was a boy. We asked him, How could he feel gay when he was no longer paying us our salaries, and how could he justify it to his conscience? He liked our mocking, and limped away from us with a rheumatic

easing of his weight from one foot to another: a figure
pathetic now that it has gone the way to dusty death, and
dear to memory through benefactions unalloyed by one
unkindness.

STUDY OF THOMAS BAILEY ALDRICH
AT PONKAPOG

Released from editorial duties, Aldrich remained in
Boston and its neighborhood, — not "genuine Boston"
himself, as Mr. Greenslet tells us he liked to say, "but
Boston plated," — and wrought faithfully at his work
as a writer. From 1874 to 1881 he continued, as he had
begun, to be a prolific contributor of poems, short
stories, and novels to the *Atlantic*. When he succeeded
Mr. Howells in the later of these two years, it was
as if in prophetic verification of the words in Professor Perry's "Park Street Papers" which carry one both
back of Aldrich's time and beyond it: —

The editors of the *Atlantic* have always been drafted
from the ranks of its contributors; mere contributors, who

once enclosed stamps for the return of manuscript and
waited and wondered if it would prove "magazinable."
How can such a one, drawn in a moment, like Browning's
conscript,

> From the safe glad rear to the dreadful van,

pretend that he has been invested with infallibility? " I
am fain to think it vivacious," wrote Lowell of a certain
Contributors' Club which he was submitting to the editor
in 1890, nearly thirty years after his own editorship
closed, "but if your judgment verify my fears, don't
scruple to return it. I can easily make other disposition of
it, or at worst there is always the waste-basket." His Club
was accepted, in spite of Lowell's fears — and, as it happened, it was his last contribution to the magazine.

Once, when Lowell was in Europe, Aldrich, for two
years, had occupied his Elmwood house in Cambridge.
His surroundings were always invested with charm.
When he came to the *Atlantic,* says Mr. Greenslet in his
biography, "even in his editorial office Aldrich con-
trived to surround himself with the homelike comfort to
which he was accustomed"; and the biographer goes
on: —

He chose for his purpose a little back room at No.
4 Park Street, reached by a spiral stairway much
resembling the pictures of Dante's Purgatorio with the
terrestrial Paradise at its summit. Its windows over-
looked that haunt of ancient peace, the Old Granary
Burying-Ground, where, as he liked to say, lay those who
would never submit any more manuscript. But any melan-
choly that might have arisen from the scenery was miti-
gated by an open fire of cannel coal, by a pipe, — an engine
which had not hitherto been in favor in that office, but
which was expressly nominated in the bond between the

editor and his publisher, — and by the constant attendance
of his setter " Trip." Once when Trip ate a sonnet, Aldrich
asked, " How did *he* know it was doggerel? "

For the manner in which his daily work was done
Mr. Greenslet evoked the memories of Miss Francis,
whose recollections of the *Atlantic* office under Fields
have already been cited; and one cannot do better in
this place than to copy again some records of this editorial assistant, who worked with Aldrich through all
the nine years of his incumbency.

The routine of the office was simple enough. The prose
manuscripts were read, sifted, commented on, and all with
the smallest degree of merit placed in a drawer which
quickly became over-full, waiting for the editor's exami-
nation on a clearing-up day, of uncertain date, when he
energetically went through the mass, and laid aside a few
for further consideration. These did not usually wait long,
for as an editor Mr. Aldrich lived from hand to mouth;
the box, in which accepted manuscripts were kept was
never very full, was often half empty. He had an unwill-
ingness to accumulate copy — for which much might be
said — as well as a fastidious taste, and was not infre-
quently a solicitor for articles. Sometimes destitution
seemed to stare him in the face, but with his usual good
fortune things altogether desirable arrived at the last
moment, and the supply never failed. The poetry I never
read, as he wished to see all that came, and his reading
was certainly quite sufficient. His judgment in the case
of verse was very quick and sure, even the single felicity
of phrase or graceful thought in a poor poem never
escaped his notice. His standard of what *Atlantic* verse
should be was high and not often to be attained to, but he
came as near to it as circumstances allowed and never
accepted poems lightly or unadvisedly. In the matter of

short stories he was nearly as critical, while a slovenly or careless style in any sort of article would almost obscure whatever other merit the paper might possess. He was, however, very fair-minded towards articles treating of subjects which did not appeal to his personal tastes, if the writers thereof were clear-headed and had a reasonable amount of literary skill. . . .

To work with him was usually a most agreeable experience, but, as to accomplishment, it had its disadvantages. It was likely to remind him of something much more interesting. Some bit of autobiography, oftenest an anecdote of his early life, which led to another and yet another. Ah, if it could be possible to put that desultory talk, vivid narration, scintillating humor, into cold type, it would leave any tale he ever told with pen and ink far behind!

Another detail of his ways as an editor appears in Mr. Howells's "Recollections of an Atlantic Editorship." After describing his own struggles with the bushel of accepted manuscript inherited from his two predecessors, a load which he gradually lightened by counting each manuscript dead when its author died, and he could lay "his unpublished manuscript like a laurel crown upon his tomb," he proceeds: "When Aldrich came to my relief, I placed a pathetic remnant of the bushel, say a half-peck, in his hands, and it was with a shock that I learned later of his acting upon a wholly different conception of his duty to these heirlooms; he sent them all back, dead or alive, and so made an end of an intolerable burden."

In the following terms Mr. Greenslet has summarized the results of Aldrich's work as an *Atlantic* editor: —

Whatever were his alternations of mood and easy-going methods, Aldrich made an excellent magazine for the

lettered reader. Under his conduct the *Atlantic* attained
a notable unity of tone and distinction of style. A little
less accessible to new and unknown talent than Mr. Howells
had been, he was yet quick to perceive the note of distinction, and few of his swans turned out geese. He was not
a militant editor, and was not greatly concerned about
politics and affairs. His interest was first and always
literature, and perhaps no editor of the *Atlantic* printed
more of it. During his tenure of office the afterglow of
the great day of New England literature was fading, but
fading slowly. He could count on occasional poems from
Longfellow, Holmes, Whittier, and Lowell, to say nothing
of the younger group headed by Sill. He had Parkman
and Fiske for historical papers; James, Helen Hunt Jack-
son, Miss Murfree, Mrs. Oliphant, Marion Crawford, Miss
Jewett, and the two Hardys, American and English, for
fiction. He developed the critical department of the magazine to a high degree of competence by marshaling what
has seldom been seen in this country, a thoroughly com-
pact and capable coterie of critical reviewers. This group,
which was composed of Richard Grant White, G. E. Wood-
berry, George Parsons Lothrop, Horace Scudder, and Miss
Harriet Waters Preston, contributed a surprisingly large
proportion of the material that is embodied in the score of
volumes of his editing. Read to-day, after the lapse of
twenty years, it is still remarkable for penetration of in-
sight and felicity of expression. It was under Aldrich, too,
that the *Atlantic* won its international reputation as
being, in the phrase of an English review, "the best edited
magazine in the English language." To his fastidious
sense of phrase and syntax, reading proof was a sacra-
ment. If he habitually delegated the celebration of it to
his assistant, his interest in the result was none the less
keen, and it fared ill with any split infinitive or suspended
nominative — even with such seemingly innocent locutions
as "several people" — that fell under his searching eye.
The editorial letters that Aldrich wrote out in his beau-

tiful round hand are models of terse and luminous expression, and many of his younger writers remember their
helpfulness with sincere gratitude. With all his contributors, both known and unknown, he was something of a
martinet, particularly in the matter of the pruning away of
longueurs; but both classes soon came to trust his editorial
acumen and literary craftsmanship. The books in which
his correspondence was copied are fruitful reading for the
magazine writer, professional or amateur.

His own view of one important service of the *Atlantic*
was expressed in a private letter, not hitherto quoted
in print, to the writer of an historical sketch of the
magazine, published in the Fortieth Anniversary number, in 1897. " I am sorry that the *Atlantic*," he wrote,
" did not put in its claim to being the father of the short
story. Of course there were excellent short stories before the *Atlantic* was born — Poe's and Hawthorne's
— but the magazine gave the short story a place which
it had never before reached. It began with ' The Dia-
mond Lens ' of Fitz-James O'Brien, and ended with —
well, it has not ended yet."

As a revisitant of his editorial haunts, Aldrich
makes the following apparition in Professor Perry's
" Park Street Papers " : —

For many years he had been wont to visit more or less
regularly the editorial room which still claimed his name
and fame as one of its treasured possessions. Perched
upon the edge of a chair as if about to take flight, he would
often linger by the hour, to the delight of his listeners.
His caustic art played around every topic of conversation.
He did not disdain the veriest " shop talk " concerning
printers' errors and the literary fashions of the hour.
" Look at those boys ! " he exclaimed once, as he picked up

an illustrated periodical containing the portraits of a couple of that month's beardless novelists. " When I began to write, we waited twenty years before we had our portraits printed, but nowadays these young fellows have themselves photographed before they even sit down to write their book." Himself a fastidious composer and reviser, Mr. Aldrich was severely critical of current magazine literature. " That was a well-written essay," he once said of an *Atlantic* contribution which he liked, "but you will find that he used a superfluous 'of' upon the second page." . . . More than once I have heard him declare that he would have rejected Mr. Kipling's "Recessional" if it had been offered to the *Atlantic*—so extreme was his dislike for one or two harsh lines in that justly celebrated poem. The one American poem which he would have most liked to write, was, he said, Emerson's "Bacchus"— where, amid inimitable felicities, there are surely harsh lines enough.

It was indeed, in the maintenance and reinforcement of the strictest literary traditions of the *Atlantic*— traditions both of workmanship and of spirit—that Aldrich rendered his peculiar service to the magazine. Not of the "reformer type" himself, like Lowell, "he cared no more," in the words of Professor Perry, "for the practical later phases of transcendentalism than for the earlier speculative ones"; and he never lost "his engaging air of detachment from New England's cherished enterprises." Yet on occasion there could appear in his personal dealings a vigor quite foreign to the dilettante: witness, for example, the instance of the ill-regulated contributor who on receipt of a "declination with thanks," retorted: "My robust nature abhors your disgusting duplicity. You are a vulgar unblushing Rascal and an impudent audacious *Liar*. . . . You ought to be publicly horsewhipped. Nothing would gratify me more than to give you a sounder thrashing than *you have yet received.*" Aldrich preserved the letter, with a neatly penciled note thereon: "The gentleman with the 'robust nature' was politely invited to call at No. 4 Park Street on any day that week between 9 A.M. and 3 P.M., but the 'robust nature' failed to materialize." If the meeting had taken place, Aldrich would certainly not have impaired the broad applicability of the lines which Dr. Henry Van Dyke addressed to him on his seventieth birthday: —

> You've done your work with careful, loving touch, —
> An artist to the very core of you,—
> You've learned the magic spell of " not too much ";
> We read, — and wish that there was more of you.

Aldrich was not an autobiographical person, nor was Scudder, who succeeded him in 1890 and held the editorship of the magazine — actively, until 1896, when Mr. Walter H. Page became associated with its conduct and assumed many of its labors; nominally until 1898, when Mr. Page succeeded to the post both in fact and in name. For the present purpose it is unfortunate, moreover, that the fifth editor of the *Atlantic* has not been the theme, like all his predecessors, of biography and reminiscence. There is no fund of written record concerning him or by him upon which to draw. This may be ascribed to the fact that he was primarily an editor — not primarily a poet, novelist, public figure, though, even as they who came before him, essentially a man of letters. He was, besides, an editor whose work, with an extraordinary unity of faithfulness, was done for a single publishing house, or, more strictly, for that succession of firms from which in 1880 emerged the firm of Houghton, Mifflin & Company.

In the issuance of periodicals Scudder had served an early apprenticeship as editor of the *Riverside Magazine for Young People,* published by H. O. Houghton & Co. Well within the first decade of the *Atlantic* he appeared among its contributors both of verse and of fiction, each of a delicate quality presaging a keen perception of the *dulce* in writing, even after his production of the *utile* had come to engage all his own efforts. In later life he wrote to his friend, Henry M. Alden, of *Harpers' Magazine,* of a "former state of existence when we were poets"; and said of the change that came to him: "I woke to find myself at the desk of a literary workman." From 1872 he made a three-years' experiment of membership in the Houghton firm, but dropped with relief the more commercial interests of publishing. The manufacture and sale of books concerned him less than the earlier processes of their making.

One of his valuable labors in these younger days was to prepare, in 1876, the first comprehensive index of the *Atlantic,* covering its first twenty years. Opposite his own name, twenty-eight contributions are entered, chiefly reviews. The later indexes show this number vastly increased. His unacknowledged work for what he delighted to call "the house" was legion — voluminous and sympathetic long-hand correspondence with authors; deft and enlightening introductions to single volumes; series of books planned and editorially executed, most notably, perhaps, that "Riverside Literature Series" which embodied so effectively his cherished belief that the very best of reading was none too good for those whose taste was still in process of formation. In this field of education he was indeed among the pioneers. A trustee of Williams College, of which

HORACE ELISHA SCUDDER
Fifth Editor of the *Atlantic Monthly*
1890–1898

he was a graduate, he held the cause of education among his strongest personal interests, and seized every opportunity to forward it through all the means afforded by his connection with an influential publishing house and with the *Atlantic*.

No less naturally, then, than Aldrich, did Scudder step into the editorship of the *Atlantic*. It was the best editorial position in the gift of his "house," and when it fell vacant, to whom but to Scudder, the most faithful and practised of editors, should it be offered?

If the eight years of his editorship may be said to mark the climax of the magazine's identification with the firm which published it, this was more intrinsic than apparent in the pages of the *Atlantic*. They reflected, probably more than ever before, an editor's personal interest in education. Otherwise the magazine was much as it had been; for what Professor Perry has said of Aldrich's time was only a little less true of Scudder's; "It was before the day of wild west feats of editorial chase, capture, and exhibition"; and Scudder, content, as some of his predecessors had been, to take chiefly, and gratefully, what came to him, left to his successors the full development of editorial initiative through invitation.

The years of his editorship were none the less years of extraordinary industry. When he took charge of the *Atlantic* he did not drop his work as literary director of the firm's book-publishing enterprises, but only added the new to the old labors. An assistant recalls Scudder's coming to his desk on one of this "new hand's" first days in the editorial office, and depositing thereon some ten or eleven volumes of a new edition of Thoreau, in page proofs, with a request for an index of the entire set. "I always like to keep some knitting-work of that kind on hand myself," said the indefatigable chief, as if in token of the standard of industry to which the members of his office family were expected to attain. What he looked for in others he demanded inexorably of himself. It was he, rather than any one of his editorial helpers, who sped out of the office late in the afternoon bearing a huge green-baize bag stuffed with books and manuscripts, bespeaking more than knitting-work in the evening, and sped back with it at an early morning hour, ready for a long and cheerful day of work. Into its busy hours he could crowd the writing, the highly skillful and competent writing, of many of the "Comments on New Books" to which the later pages of the *Atlantic* were then devoted. There was always time for friendly consultations with contributors, for encouragement to promising beginners, for suggesting directions to be followed by more practised hands. In that variable fraction of an editor's work which consists of giving freely of his time and thought to the writers who most need such help, Scudder was indeed a liberal giver. The essential goodness of the man, the true kindness of his heart, made him a friend dearly prized and remembered by many. The *Atlantic,* from which he retired, a man of sixty years, in 1898, had given expression, not only to the devoted nature of its editor, but also to the most distinctive inheritances of its two-score years.

V

Scudder was the last of the *Atlantic* editors who belonged, even as a younger contemporary, to the group of writers which dominated the magazine through its earlier years. With him an era in the history of the magazine may be said to have come to an end. The full score of years since his retirement belongs essentially to our own day. As this is not the place for a contemporaneous history of the magazine, or for weighing the work of men whose activities are, happily, still unfinished, it will suffice in a few remaining pages to make a hasty survey of the personal forces which have directed the course of the magazine since 1896.

In that year Mr. Walter Hines Page, whose services as United States Ambassador to Great Britain from 1913 to 1918 have recently brought him to an honored central place on the stage of the world, began his association with the *Atlantic*. A native of North Carolina, educated in the South, he represented even more than Mr. Howells, with his Ohio background, and Aldrich, on whom the influences of New Orleans and New York had made his New England birth seem almost an accident, the identification of the *Atlantic* with America rather than with any section of it. For five years before becoming, in 1895, a literary adviser to the firm of Houghton, Mifflin & Co., he had been editor of the *Forum* in New York. A deep interest in national affairs, finding its outlet both in this magazine and, from 1900 to 1913, in his editorship of the *World's Work,* gave a stronger color to the political aspect of the *Atlantic* than any previous editor had imparted to it. His term of service,

From a painting by Lazlo, by courtesy of *The World's Work*

WALTER HINES PAGE
Sixth Editor of the *Atlantic Monthly*
1898 – 1899

the three years from 1896 to 1899, through two of which the titular editorship remained with Scudder, though absent for many months in Europe, was the shortest of all the editorships of the magazine — Lowell, with his four years, standing next in order of brevity. But, like all the editors who had preceded him, he left his clear individual imprint on its pages, the definite work of a powerful personality which had for its chief concern the problems of our national life.

To him succeeded, in 1899, Professor Bliss Perry, a native of Western Massachusetts, educated at Williams College and German universities, a professor of English at Princeton at the time his editorship began, the holder of a similar chair at Harvard before it ended. In him also was embodied a larger American interest than that which derives its special suffusion of tint from the dome of the State House in Boston. During the ten years of his editorship, the interest of letters received the emphasis which might have been expected; but it seems more than fortuitous that the first honorary doctorate conferred upon him was that of L.H.D., for the "more humane letters" were surely his chief concern as editor.

A later historian of the *Atlantic* will be sure to draw freely upon the volume of "Park Street Papers," in which Professor Perry has brought together the "Prologues" with which he made it his custom, as "toastmaster" at the *Atlantic's* board, to open, in January numbers of the magazine, the annual feast for which he was responsible. Here a single fragment will serve the twofold purpose of illustrating Professor Perry's conception of his task and of the place for such a periodical as the *Atlantic* in American life: —

BLISS PERRY
Seventh Editor of the *Atlantic Monthly*
1899–1909

If the *Atlantic Monthly* were a repository; if it confined itself to the discussion of Roman antiquities, or the sonnets of Wordsworth, or the planting of the colony of Massachusetts Bay, no one but the specialists would concern themselves with the opinions expressed in its pages. But it happens to be particularly interested in this present world; curious about the actual conditions of politics and society, of science and commerce, of art and literature. Above all, it is engrossed with the lives of the men and women who are making America what it is and is to be.

With notable success Professor Perry gave ten years to the realization of this humanistic ideal. If it has seemed unsuitable to deal in detail with the achievements of recent editors, it would be even less possible in these pages to recount and appraise the work of the present management of the magazine. A few facts, however, should be given.

In the summer of 1908, when Professor Perry was planning to free himself from editorial responsibilities, it happened that the publishers of the magazine were facing the problems of a general rearrangement of their business organization. At that moment an opportunity to part with the *Atlantic* on terms assuring the continuance of its historic place in American life presented itself. Mr. Ellery Sedgwick, then of New York, where he had given himself a rigorous training in the editing and publishing of periodicals, proposed to establish the Atlantic Monthly Company, under his presidency, and to acquire the magazine, to be conducted under his editorship, with Mr. MacGregor Jenkins, long associated with the magazine in the office of Houghton, Mifflin & Company, as publisher. This offer was accepted, and in August, 1908, the *Atlantic* began to appear under the new auspices. For the first time since the days of James T. Fields the editor was directly concerned with the publishing success of the magazine. As it found favor with a larger and larger public, the business of the company responsible for it expanded, by the acquisition of two other periodicals, — first the *House Beautiful,* then the *Living Age,* established by E. Littell in 1844, — and also through the publication of books bearing the imprint of the Atlantic Monthly Press. Thus the magazine has come to stand at the centre instead of the circumference of the circle of interests with which it is associated.

In the summer of 1918, the new company celebrated its tenth anniversary with a dinner, which differed from the old *Atlantic* feasts chiefly through the absence of all contributors and the presence of all the men and women, employers and employed, more than fifty in number, who are actively engaged in the daily work of the corporation. Certain things may be said under cover of rhyme which are inappropriate to matter-of-fact prose. It may, therefore, be permitted to print the following verses which were read on that occasion: —

AN ATLANTIC PORT

No harborside of mystery, where silent troops set sail,
No secret haven for the saved along the U-boat's trail—
A happier roadstead this, wherein are sunk all doubts and fears,
The safe Atlantic anchorage — the Port of Ten New Years!

The good ship bears an ocean's name — the ocean on whose breast
Our fathers, brave adventurers all, fared forth into the west —
Across whose leagues our flower of gallant youth now eastward
fare,
Beneath the flag of human-kind a comrade's part to bear.

Like to the sea itself the ship, with healing on its wings,
Fresh spirit to the wearied, fresh hope and courage, brings;
Yet bounded by no shore it sails — o'er city, hill and plain,
Borne on an ever-rising tide — a new Atlantic main!

Full fifty years its argosies sailed monthly forth in pride —
The spoils of all our Samarcands bulging the vessel's side;
Yet sails were growing obsolete, far lands lay unexplored,
Fresh voyages beckoned when a new young captain stepped on
    board.

The rivets all he tightened, to sail-power added steam,
Installed new turbine engines, extended length and beam,
Signed year by year a growing crew — mates, seamen, yeomen,
    brave —
Yeowomen, too! — and sailed, yeo-ho! out on the rolling wave!

Letters of marque the ship bore none; yet prizes struck their
    flags,
Calling, "We'd sail with you before our banners are in rags!" —
Strange caravels, and quaintly named, as from some mythic
    age—
The "Houseboat Beautiful" came first, and then the "Living
    Wage!"

So grows the squadron, one by one, with small boats, shaped
    like books,
Swarming about, with lines austere, or gallant, or *de luxe!*
So may it great and greater grow, while landsmen swell their
    cheers
For captain, mates, and crew, moored now in the Port of Ten
    New Years!

A final word must be said to link together the *Atlantic* of the present and of the past. The magazine
defined itself at the very beginning as "Devoted to
Literature, Art and Politics." That devotion, embrac-
ing the "Science" which for some time was interpolated
between "Literature" and "Art," has remained una-

bated through all the changes and chances of more than
sixty years. The magazine has never called itself a
mirror, but that is what it has always been, or tried to
be — a mirror reflecting whatever has most vitally concerned the life of the nation and its thinking citizens
through six eventful decades. In the first of these a
great war cast its shadow across the face of America.
The shadow, and many glorious lights which it caused
to stand out but the more clearly, were reflected in the
Atlantic's mirror. In the sixth decade another and a
vastly fiercer war has darkened the face of all the
world. The reflection of it in a great variety of its
infinitely complex phases has been precisely as characteristic of the *Atlantic* to-day as the poems and war
papers of the sixties were characteristic of the magazine in that period. It is an utterly different world in
which we have come to live, and the paths of many
of its quests lead into new and different fields; but the
men and women who inhabit it have much in common
with the essential nature of their grandfathers and
grandmothers. Clothes and houses, means of communi-
cation and transportation, external trappings of every
kind, have changed in a thousand ways. The physical
form and spiritual content of the *Atlantic* have been
modified rather than altered to meet the demands of a
new day. Like the hearts and minds which are the best
possession of our country, the magazine has truly represented one of the constant elements in the life of the
nation.

An incident of the past summer is significant. A
friend of the *Atlantic* was traveling from Chicago to
New York on the Twentieth Century Limited. The
smoking-car in which he sat contained perhaps a dozen
men reading magazines. The most distinguished of them

in outward appearance—perhaps the president of a
bank, thought the observer, if not of a university—was
deep in the perusal of *Snappy Stories*. Another man,
of rat-like mien, buried himself in the *Wall Street
Journal*. All the other ten were reading the *Atlantic*.
One of them interrupted himself from time to time by
drawing pencil lines around certain passages. The
Atlantic's friend had the curiosity to stroll down the
aisle, and let his eye fall upon one of the marked pages.
The title above it was "Religion in War-Time."

It has never been other than a pitiable mistake to
believe that the best of Americans are indifferent to
the issues of life and death. They do not ask, or wish,
constantly to be confronted with them, stark and solitary; there is ample room in their scheme of things for
the humors and graces of living. But one likes to think
of the reader of "Religion in War-Time" — also of the
other nine. These wayfaring Americans, typical of
many thousands of their countrymen, now stand on the
threshold of a new era. Peace succeeds to war, the
processes of reconstruction must follow those of disrup-
tion. Men and women of open mind and heart, ready
for every effort to seize upon what is best in the fateful
future, face it with a confidence in which the *Atlantic*
shares.

Entrance to present offices
41 Mt. Vernon Street

THE TWENTY-ONE TITLES INCLUDED IN THIS LIST SEEM
ASSURED, BY UNIVERSAL CONSENT, OF A PERMA-
NENT PLACE IN LITERATURE.

ALDRICH — Marjorie Daw (*January*, 1873).

BROWNING — Prospice (*May*, 1864).

CLEMENS — Old Times on the Mississippi (*January–
June, August*, 1875).

EMERSON — Days (*November*, 1857).

HALE — The Man without a Country (*November*, 1863).

HARTE — How Santa Claus came to Simpson's Bar
(*March* 1872).

HOLMES — The Autocrat of the Breakfast Table (including "The Chambered Nautilus" and
"The Wonderful One Hoss Shay.") (*November, 1857– October*, 1858).

MRS. HOWE — The Battle Hymn of the Republic (*February*, 1862)

HOWELLS — The Lady of the Aroostook (*November,
1878– March*, 1879).

H. JAMES, JR. — Daisy Miller (*April–June*, 1883).

W. JAMES — Talks to Teachers on Psychology (*February–May*, 1899).

MISS JEWETT — The Country of the Pointed Firs (*January, March, July, September*, 1896).

KIPLING — The Disturber of Traffic (*September*, 1891).

LONGFELLOW — The Children's Hour (*September*, 1860).
Paul Revere's Ride (*January*, 1861).

LOWELL — Commemoration Ode (*September*, 1865).
Biglow Papers (*January–June*, 1862; *February*, 1863; *April*, 1865; *May*, 1866).

MOODY — Ode in Time of Hesitation (*April*, 1900).

PARKMAN — Wolfe on the Plains of Abraham (*September*, 1884).

SILL — A Fool's Prayer (*April*, 1879).

WHITTIER — Barbara Frietchie (*October*, 1863).

INDEX

ALDEN, HENRY M., 89.

ALDRICH, THOMAS BAILEY, *fourth editor,* editor of *Every Saturday,* 52, 79; relations with Lowell and Fields as editors 77, 78; succeeds Howells, 81; as editor, Miss Francis, Howells, and Greenslet quoted concerning, 83, 84; as a revisitant of the editorial haunts 86; 55, 69, 72, 93.

Anthony, Mr. 55.

Apthorp, W. F., 70.

Atlantic Club, memorable meeting of, described by T. W. Higginson, 20 *ff.*

ATLANTIC MONTHLY, foundation of 13 *ff.*; named by Holmes, 18, 19; contributors to first number, 24, 25, 26; anonymity of authors in, 25, 26, abandoned, 26; a success from the start, 26; its aims and policy, 26-28; sold to Ticknor & Fields, 33-35; in the Civil War, 45*ff.*; in the Franco-Prussian and Spanish wars, 49; the "True Story of Lady Byron's Life," and its effect, 49-51; successive owners of, 51, 52; its home on Tremont St., 52 *ff.*; original music printed in, 70; origin of the "Contributors' Club," 71; "the best edited magazine in the English language, 85; and the short story, 86; the present and the past, 99-101.

Atlantic Monthly Company, 51, 97.

Atlantic Monthly Press, 98.

"Atlantic Port, An," 98.

Barrett, Lawrence, 69.

Beecher, Henry Ward, 31.

Boston Fire, 57.

Boott, Francis, 70.

Brown, John, 46.

Browning, Robert, his "Prospice," 47.

Buck, Dudley, 70.

Byron, George Gordon, Lord, 49.

Byron, Lady, the "True Story" of her life, 49-51.

Cabot, James Elliot, 13, 15.

Civil War, the, and the *Atlantic,* 45 *ff.*

Claflin, William, 72.

Clemens, Samuel L., his first contribution to the *Atlantic,* 67; his famous speech at the Whittier dinner, 73-75.

Clough, Arthur Hugh, 26, 45.

Contributors' Club, founded by Howells, 71.

Craddock, Charles Egbert. *See* Murfree, Mary N.

Crawford, F. Marion, 85.

Curtis, George William, quoted, 40.

Dinner-parties, and the early history of the *Atlantic,* 19 *ff.*; reviewed in later years, 72.

Dodge, Mary A., *A Battle of the Books,* quoted, 58.

Eichberg, Julius, 70.

Emerson, Ralph Waldo, contributes to first number, 24; his poem, "Days," 25; quoted, on the practice of anonymity, 25; his article, "Books," criticized, 30; his "The President's Proclamation," 45, and "Voluntaries," 47; his Bacchus," 87; 13, 15, 55, 63, 73, 74.

Every Saturday, 52, 79, 80.

Felton, Cornelius C., 28.

Fielding, Henry, his *Tom Jones,* 24.

FIELDS, JAMES T., *second editor,* succeeds Lowell, 34, 37; as a publisher, 39, 40, 41; as editor, T. W. Higginson quoted, concerning, 42-45; his *Yesterdays*

McGrath-Sherrill Press, Boston